SILHOUETTE OF SORROW

Silhouette of Sorrow

A shared journey through loss and grief

S J Wynne-Hughes

Copyright © Susanne J Wynne-Hughes 2018
All rights reserved. No part of this publication may be reproduced, stored in a retrieval system or transmitted in any form by any means, electronic, mechanical, photocopying, recording or otherwise, without the prior written permission of the publisher and copyright holder. Susanne Wynne-Hughes asserts the moral right to be identified as the author of this work.

Published by Susanne Wynne-Hughes

Typeset by BookPOD

ISBN: 978-0-6483120-0-0 (pbk)
eISBN: 978-0-6483120-1-7 (ebook)

For my father
His love and kindness
&
To the faithful friends
whose never failing love
supported me through this journey

Appreciations

Cover by Andrew Kopp, a professional photographer and friend who also photographed the images in the book.

Gratitude to the Flinders Literary Arts Group (FLAG) for sponsoring the writing workshop with Sian Prior that fostered my interest in writing.

Appreciation to Sian Prior for her lively tuition in refining my memoir.

Thanks to my generous friends for suggestions on drafts of the manuscript: Rob Eldridge, Jenny Armstrong, Clyth Hoult, Rhonda Galbally, Kip Turner, Alex Stewart and to Kate McDonough for typing my first manuscript.

Thank you to Tony Moore for his kindness, encouragement and guidance as my book mentor.

Jigsaw Pieces

PART ONE: LOSS

My Red Trees 13
One Tuesday 20
Thursday 23
Sunday Celebration 26
Aftermath 33
My Empty Chair 38
Musical Memories 40
My Silhouette 43
Together or Apart 47
Respite 51
Seeking Help 55
Couple Envy 59
Restless 62
Compounding Grief 65
Vulnerability 71
The Last Year 73
A Plea 79

PART TWO: CONNECTIONS

Searching 87
Lessons Learned from Dad 94
Bereavement Bonding 99
Travel Traumas and Triumphs 105
The Bluestone Decades 114
Code of Female Friendship 146
Friendship Circles 148
A Stepping Stone 154
Letting Go 160
Creativity 163
Partnering 169
Finding 177
Ashes to Ashes 178

About the Author 180

PART ONE

Loss

My Red Trees

I have painted two trees red in my life, both on Christmas Eve. The first tree was in Red China in 1979. The second tree was painted in Red Hill in 2014 after I paid a visit to the police station to dispose of the gun my husband Michael used to kill himself.

Every year we travelled overseas at Christmas time into exotic countries to experience the colour and culture of different places; we had been to Morocco, Bolivia, Laos, Indonesia and Mexico. This allowed us to miss out on the synthetic Santa Claus stupidity at home. The Christmas in China was different, as we did celebrate with Santa. It was 1979 and China was just opening up to the West. We were staying on the outskirts of Beijing where the locals had rarely encountered Westerners before. At this time you could only travel in a group whose program was tightly controlled and supervised. No wandering off by ourselves. Our group consisted of American and Japanese students plus five Australians on an adventure.

Michael was very hairy. He had a long beard and a bush of curly shoulder-length hair and wherever we went the locals cried out 'Karl Marx'. On Christmas Eve the locals asked us to put on a pantomime for the thousand onlookers who were coming to witness a Christian Christmas celebration. It was being held in the banquet ballroom of the rather dilapidated Russian-built hotel where we were staying. This was surrounded by wide verandas so hordes could be squeezed in to witness our action. With all that hair, Michael was the obvious choice to play Santa Claus. He was pleased to be dressed up in red clothes and have his hair and beard coated in white talcum powder. It was a happy time in our lives. Santa did plenty of 'ho, ho, ho' with a sack on his back.

My task was painting and decorating the Christmas tree. With my bucket of red paint I started with the trunk first, then the top branches and fronds. Fortunately I was outside as the red paint dripped like Aussie gum sap from a wound and then turned into icicles.

With the help of our guide, in a local shop we had found little ornaments to decorate the tree. Our guide explained the Chinese mythology about these ornaments.

They were colourful carvings in the shape of a tree with a dragon representing immortality and a red phoenix. They were called the Tree of Life. The guide explained there is a Taoist legend of that magical peach tree that produces a peach every 3000 years and the person who eats the fruit receives immortality. We carefully threaded the carvings onto the branches of our Christmas tree, which made it look festive and fun. As the final touch I placed a big red Chairman Mao star on top of the tree.

As part of the pantomime we were also asked to perform and sing for our Chinese onlookers. Michael and I composed a song we called 'Walking the Long March' which we sang with the other Australians to the tune of 'Waltzing Matilda'. The Gang of Four were still in power at the time and we took a risk with the lyrics, hoping none of the Chinese audience members spoke English. I recently rediscovered the original song written on parchment notepaper.

This song shows how irreverent, foolhardy and perhaps pioneering we were.

WALKING THE LONG MARCH

Once a jolly comrade camped on a commune
Under the shade of Chairman Mao
And he sang as he watched and waited for his next maotai
You'll come a walking the long march with me
Walking the long march
Walking the long march
You'll come a walking the long march with me
And he sang as he watched and waited for his next maotai
You'll come a walking the long march with me
Up jumped the Gang of 4
Pushing out their new hard line
Oh what a bore, what a bore, Gang of 4
Where's that jolly maotai you've got in your knapsack
You'll come a walking the long march with me.

For those of you who have not been to China, let me share that maotai is a fiery drink, smells a bit like methylated spirits and tastes worse. At the Christmas banquet we were encouraged to drink it and each time I tipped mine out, it was quickly replenished. It was awful stuff but we didn't know the language or etiquette to stop it being served.

It was fortunate that none of the locals spoke English so we were not in grave trouble with the words of our song. Santa was digging into his sack and giving gifts to some of the local children, with me acting as his helper. We were quite a sight because my long natural blonde hair and red clothes complemented Santa's outfit. The onlookers clapped with joy. The red flags waved in the air as the locals thanked us for our pantomime. The colour red in China is a symbol of good luck.

The second time I painted a tree red though, I was feeling anything but lucky. It was early morning on Christmas Eve three years after Michael died, when the police rang asking me to collect my property that day! The 'property' consisted of the gun Michael had used, and his antidepressant medication. The officer who rang me explained this property could now be released because the Coroner had finally completed the report on the cause of death. This three-year time delay had occurred because I had given permission for Michael's case to be part of a study dealing with the role of health professionals in the firearms licensing process. Maybe lessons could be learned.

That afternoon on Christmas Eve, I parked the car. I sat for a while. Six deep breaths. I found myself in front of the unwelcoming facade of the police station. Its steely structures shouted the voice of 'authority'. The station was a hub of activity on that Christmas Eve afternoon with a crowd of other forlorn visitors who, like me, were probably wishing they were anywhere but in the waiting room of a police station.

I gave the police sergeant my name and he said, 'You have come here about a gun; which gun club do you belong to?' Before I could reply, he added, 'I go to the Frankston Gun Club each week and it's a great place to spend time with other gun enthusiasts.'

'The gun is not mine. It was my husband's,' I told him.

'Have you come to collect it for him?' he asked.

'No, my husband used it to kill himself and I do not want it,' I replied.

'You could sell it,' he suggested. I just stared loudly at him. Then he looked at the file down on the counter and his face changed. 'Sorry for my confusion. I see here in the paperwork you want to dispose of the gun.'

Being chatty doesn't always mean you are being compassionate. This policeman clearly had no idea about the history of the case or me. If only he knew that prison officers at work thought I had a 'good eye' for the target at the rifle range when I learned to use a firearm.

How on earth had Michael been able to obtain a gun licence? My anger came shooting back at me and the tissues were out again.

'Could I please just sign the paperwork to destroy the gun?' I said, without looking at him. 'I don't want to sell it because someone else may use it to harm themselves or others.'

I signed the piece of paper, left the police station and scurried to the safety of home.

I needed cheering up. Painting and designing have always been my consolation. I had been to Bunnings earlier that week to buy a tin of red paint for my beautiful dead plum tree. It had such a lovely shape and red had been my favourite colour since my childhood. Last season the tree had rich, juicy plums but something mysterious had seen it wilt and wither. Attempts to save it were fruitless. Maybe it was the same for Michael. To most people he looked fine on the outside but inside he was struggling with his despair. If only I had known that he had decided he could no longer cope with his pain and anxiety.

On the night of the police visit I went out with my tin of red paint and into the orchard with my ladder. Tackling a symmetrical tree that was a metre tall and two metres wide made me reflect about painting my first tree red all those years ago in China. My emotional energy went into gardening gear studying the shape and angles of the tree. Living with Michael and his demons had taken a toll on both of us.

Painting my second tree red in Red Hill some thirty-five years later on a Christmas Eve, I smiled rather than sang. It touched my heart painting my beautiful dead tree red, and I hoped in time maybe joy and playfulness would return to me.

Red China, red trees, Red Hill reminded me about Ruby Red who came into my life as a child, an imaginary friend. After I painted my tree I wrote this poem about my memories of her.

RUBY RED
Here's a thing about Red
Some say as a colour red signifies fire and blood
Strength, power, passion and love
When I was a child red was my colour
Little dresses hats and toys
Ruby Red my imaginary friend
Came into my life when I was sad
My beloved cat Fleabag was killed
Run over by a car
Smells of burning rubber on the road
Blood everywhere
Fleabag was still warm in my arms
Loss touched me for the first time in my life
Ruby Red was a comfort to me
She shared my hurt and pain
We buried Fleabag in the garden
Lovingly planted a red rose bush for her

SILHOUETTE OF SORROW

It was my 4th birthday
I loved Ruby Red and our talks
She was wise and kind and listened
She was the answers to my questions
Other times we just played together
My brother and sister had disappeared to school
But Ruby Red was always there for me
I still feel her
When my red roses bloom each spring.

One Tuesday

He died on a Tuesday. Why would I remember this detail? I know because the Red Hill Bridge Club stopped playing cards on that Tuesday night as soon as they heard the news about Michael. My close friends came to give me a hug. What did they think? Did they know Michael had reneged on life because his pain was too great?

My friend Helen Davison found Michael's body with the gun in his lap. Minutes later I arrived to find paramedics and police officers were swarming around our property. Michael was dead in his favourite leather chair with our beloved cat, Lily, sitting on his lap. I was on the deck looking through the windows at him.

'This is a crime scene,' the young female police officer said. She was like a gatekeeper from the deck into our house. 'You cannot go in.'

I strode past and said, 'This is our house, he is my husband and I need to say good-bye to him.'

In death Michael's skin was alabaster and cold to the touch. I held his hand in the flesh for the last time, feeling the cool metal of his wedding ring in my fingers. He was dressed in clothes I loved to see him wear. His navy blue woolly jumper and navy corduroy pants matched his worn latticed Italian leather shoes. I marvelled at the fact there was no blood.

'Just one shot,' the police officer piped up. Michael was

an econometrician and the mathematics of killing himself was an exacting science. He would have studied the angles, the probabilities, the physics of how to do it cleanly.

I felt numb and hollow inside. Everything rattled. What desperation had taken him away from us? A question from the police officer ricocheted off the reality that I was still sitting with Michael. Helen was outside on the deck.

'When did you last talk to your husband?' she asked.

'Two days ago,' I replied. Then there were more questions being fired at me – how, when, why? In a blur somehow I gagged back responses.

Some more of my friends had arrived at the house and we watched as the police and ambulance prepared for their departure. Michael and his organs were going somewhere.

'His body will be taken to the morgue to determine if an autopsy is necessary as to the cause of Michael's death,' the police officer said.

'Michael is a registered organ donor, if you need my permission,' I told him. Then they were gone. My friends, Helen and her husband Frank, took me to their home.

As darkness fell, people arrived at Frank and Helen's house in ones, twos and threes until there were some fifty friends and family gathered there. Each one hugged me as they arrived. A box of tissues was handy as each hug had a different history of how we were connected. The clink of wine glasses and the smells of spicy food wafted around me. I ate and drank nothing but sat listening to those warm voices of friends and family.

As a social worker I'd had dealings with many vulnerable people struggling with grief and loss. But this time the vulnerability was mine. I was stained by sadness on that Tuesday night. I couldn't get rid of the image of the gun in Michael's lap with Lily curled around. I wept and then was submerged with tears. As I was lost to sleep from exhaustion at Frank and Helen's place, I wondered how I could get through the days ahead. Yet I was relieved that Michael's despair had ended.

Would my past experiences of loss brace me for what was to come?

It wasn't self-pity. I didn't feel like a victim even though others might see me this way. Somehow, in the safety of my circle of friends that night, I felt deeply loved.

Thursday

A few days later I was attending a wake at a winery in Red Hill for an old friend, John Varley. It was crowded and a band was playing as John had been a talented musician and viola player. Drinks were plentiful and the ill-named 'finger food' was being handed around. It was here I was approached by Jill Jones, an old acquaintance I had not seen in years. We talked about the death of our mutual friend John. She remarked it was a coincidence that John and Michael died in the same week. John had been my first boyfriend.

Jill asked, 'How and why had Michael committed suicide?'

I froze at the question. Committed. What a word. It implies suicide is a crime. I had worked for years in prisons. The prisoners in custody had been found by the courts to have committed crimes that often hurt others. That's why they were in custody. Michael had not committed a crime; he had made a personal choice.

Before I could respond to her question, she started telling me a story of a friend who had hanged herself, and how difficult it was for her husband who found her. I disappeared into the crowd. The tissue box was out again because I wanted comfort not a suicide story. It reminded me of the comforting conversations I had had with Ruby

Red, my imaginary childhood friend who had always helped me when I was sad, angry or confused.

I could have no more conversations with Michael, so perhaps another imaginary friend could be a substitute for talking to him or myself. I had always loved words, even as a child, and I still use the dictionary every day to find out meanings and the roots of words. Discovering many English words have Latin roots was a fascination of mine, probably because Latin is an unspoken or dead language.

During the week after Michael's death I learned that the Latin word for grief and sorrow was *luctus*, which helped me name my new friend. Please let me introduce you to a voice. I think the voice is a 'he'. I want to give him the name Luctus. He is the voice we all have in our heads when we talk to ourselves, especially when we are yearning for advice and guidance. He is not always welcome. It often feels as though he is intruding but I struggle to push him away. Like aberrant thoughts, he intrudes. I can't protect myself or you as the reader from him. I can't neglect him but you can. I imagine he is tall and strong, with warm brown eyes full of kindness. Listening ears and a soothing voice is my image. So our conversations began.

What an awful insensitive question from an old acquaintance. You did well to disappear into the crowd and avoid wearing her pain about the hanged friend. Maybe it would be helpful to find out the origin of the phrase 'committed suicide'. It probably relates to the time when it was a crime. Committing suicide probably reflected religious and moral objections because people saw suicide as self-murder.

My book burrowing revealed that 'an amendment of the **Crimes Act 1958**' changed the law in Victoria. Section 6A now states, 'the rule of law whereby it is a crime for a person to commit or attempt to commit suicide is abrogated.' Suicide has not been a crime in Victoria since 17 March 1967. Luctus was right.

The phrase 'committing suicide' is probably just a hangover from the past that was reinforced in the wording and language in the amendment to the law. You could tell people this if it helps lessen your annoyance and to help them understand your viewpoint. In terms of their nosy real question about how and why Michael did it, just be honest if you want to. Otherwise it is OK to say you feel vulnerable talking about it and do not tell them.

Ouch, depression and a gun might stop the why questions, but it is unlikely to stop the whispers. I overheard a woman at bridge telling her friend, 'Do you know her husband died of suicide?' Her tone made it sound shameful.

Unfortunately there is still a stigma about suicide. Unkind people might look to apportion blame on the family because for them it is shameful. This could be tough for you to deal with emotionally. Maybe practise a few responses to protect yourself.

Sunday Celebration

Five days after his death we celebrated the life of my husband, Michael Wynne-Hughes, at our property in Red Hill. A team that I call the 3937 community squad were in full flight organising the event. It was a warm sunny Sunday afternoon in December and around two hundred people gathered together to give Michael the send-off he deserved. As I scanned those assembled, I saw old faces from university days mingling with newer faces. They had all come to mourn my Michael. My love. My troubled soulmate.

I planned to deliver a eulogy for Michael. It had been therapeutic for me to write my speech. I had things I wanted to say. But it was going to be tough to deliver without breaking down. A friend, Clyth Hoult, was my back-up substitute, just in case I was overwhelmed.

Those of us who were going to speak stood on the deck looking down towards the vineyard. Friends and family were gathered below in the garden. As I was getting up to give the eulogy my knees were shaking and my heart raced. I repeated a mantra to myself – 'I want to do this.' Somehow even in my fractured state the words came out…

Dear Michael,

You and I have been married and shared our lives for the past forty years. I was attracted to you by your intellect, your rebelliousness and the fact you were a great cook. The first time I went out with you was to the theatre. Much to my mother's horror, this long haired person came to pick me up in bare feet. In her eyes this made you an unsuitable boy. I was not daunted by the fact that you were different as I was different too. Your eccentricity matched my own.

When we met, you were a Teaching Fellow in the Economics Department at Monash University. I had heard tales of you being arrested at demonstrations, and reports of your conscientious objector status when you were called up for the Vietnam War. It was a lottery where birthdates made you a potential victim or hero. You wrote an infamous song 'The Harold Holt Story' that was sung at the moratoriums in Melbourne, where we sat in Collins Street to protest against the Vietnam War. The song was sung to the tune of 'Onward Christian Soldiers' and it went like this:

> *Harold Holt get fucked for sending us to war*
> *We're not bloody going, you can bet your balls*
> *We'll not fight for conquerors, who further pollies' aims*
> *We'll not send our young men to murder and to maim*
> *Long live Ho Chi Minh.*

You and I soon teamed up and not long after began travelling the world, surviving a number of 'hairy' near-death experiences. I smile remembering what we did together.

You and I both called each other 'Bubby'. Perhaps the name was an insight because you and I never intended to have children. We believed our love for each other was enough. All nicknames embrace embarrassment. So be it.

For your 50th birthday, I had a colourful plate made which depicts all the things you loved. The plate depicts our togetherness with music, travel, tennis, bridge, cooking, wine, books, bushwalking and love. It shows your other passions, apart from me, of course. They were making jam, in the vineyard with beloved cats, map reading and sunbaking. The centrepiece of the plate is us together drinking fine wine from the duck-shaped decanter I bought for you in Paris for your 40th birthday and, of course, our beloved black cat, called 'Eartha'. You loved the fact that I always made or had made very creative presents for special times. The celebration of our love was through gifts to each other and I have fine jewellery and dresses which reflect your love.

My staff were always excited about my birthday when those wonderful big boxes arrived from Georges, the exclusive department store in Melbourne. You sent me Diane Freis dresses that you had chosen and to their and my delight you arrived at my workplace to see me wearing them.

You and I also loved playing tennis together and did so Sundays and Thursday nights for some thirty years. We were a good mixed doubles pair. Remember our system with you at the baseline and me on the net? What a team we were. You were also my bridge partner and the last time we played at Red Hill, you were pleased we won.

You were a great cook and many here today have shared your signature dishes of cassoulet, paella and the Three Birds in One where you boned a chicken, inside a goose, inside a turkey. More recently you cooked the Australian Coat of Arms of kangaroo and emu for a special pinot dinner. You were such a creative cook.

We tended our vines like children. Caring for the soil, training the vines and protecting the grapes paid dividends.

You and I have great memories of our sharing fun, food, travels with many of you who are here today.

You did not tell many people that you suffered from depression for the last twenty-five years, and during this time you struggled on and off with what we called 'your demons'. You shared them with me by our system of scores out of ten, our shorthand for how you were travelling. You had tried to end your life before and I had tried to support you through these episodes. This time you made a decision that is sad and tragic, but you ultimately made a choice because your pain and despair were too great. In spite of your illness you achieved much in both work and play which others today will share with you.

The establishment of our beloved vineyard, which we called MLF (Mike and Lew's Folly), at Eldridge Estate in 2000 was your passion. You planted those cuttings and tended those vines as your offspring. Your attention to the viticulture bore us wonderful fruit from which yummy wines were made from our first vintage in 2003. You were so proud to have the MLF 2003 pinot noir as part of the wines selected by peers to represent the Mornington Peninsula at the International Pinot Noir Celebration in 2005. Our friend David Lloyd had made the wine but when you saw your name on the program as the viticulturist, your heart leapt with joy. Mine did too for you. Seeing the wine label I had designed up there on show made us happy.

You were very keen to move to Red Hill so we rented a house for me to practise living in the country. I quickly fell in love with Red Hill because of the people. We bought this property in 2005 and it is known as MLFHQ (Mike and Lew's Folly Headquarters). We built my studio and built this house. You then embarked on establishing the vineyard and my job was the garden. My gardening coach was great and we worked together. I loved learning about plants, trees, soil and mulch and I have grown with my garden that is now flourishing. You and I did have fun creating MLFHQ.

It is hard to say when our Red Hill renaissance began, but it was probably back in the '80s, picking grapes at Main Ridge Estate. Meeting new people through the grape vines was wonderful and for us it was the beginning of many friendships. Nat and Rose White planted the first vineyard on the Mornington Peninsula and they established a wine community 'family' which welcomed and embraced us. The family still meets each Sunday night at Main Ridge Estate for drinks. It is an opportunity to gather with friends and neighbours and to find out who needs help, which is so willingly provided. We share equipment and stories and help each other out with cellar doors and all parts of the wine making process, particularly around vintage.

The day after you died friends rallied. David Lloyd and Neil and Lee Ward offered to make this year's vintage for me. How kind and generous of them. I will be calling on my mates to help with the viticulture and picking and we will make a wine this year as a tribute to you. I will call it Mike and Lew's Friends.

These past weeks have been a nightmare because you pushed me away but our great friends have been remarkable. I am fortunate to have them in my life.

I want to thank you for sharing your life with me. I loved you unconditionally and will cherish the rich experiences and memories we shared. You will always be in my heart and with me on the dining room table in the urn where your ashes will live.

You know I decoupaged the urn with images of violets we found together in Sweden. I marbled the background so it looks like the earth the violets are growing in. You would have smiled when the woman from the funeral parlour was putting your ashes in the urn, as they resembled kitty litter. Dust to dust, ashes to ashes in the urn I decorated for the first of us to die.

Thank you, Michael, for being here today in spirit which will live on.

Join us please with a glass of MLF wine to pay tribute and celebrate your life.

December 18th, 2011.

Aftermath

The day after Michael died my friends Clyth and Paul came down from Sydney to take care of me. Clyth stayed for the next three weeks. She put me in the bath and into bed each night. I felt empty and spent. Eviscerated.

There was a crush of unannounced visitors who wanted to be part of my experience. It was exhausting. Few of them had the words to help lessen my pain. 'How and why could Michael do this to you?' they asked me. I had no formula for responding. On the other hand, one wise friend wrote to me, 'Do you want me to ask if I can help ease your pain? If so, tell me how I can help.' This was the kind of language and sentiment that I found helpful. It gave me a choice and emotional space.

A week after Michael died Clyth put a large sign on the front door. *Please do not disturb. I am resting. Thank you.* After this, my front doorstep became a source of nourishment where we found food parcels, flowers and kind notes.

Michael and I had met Paul and Clyth Hoult on Dunk Island in 1980. We were all feline fanatics. Like us they saw their cats as their children and we constantly talked about them as though they were people. They were a child-free couple by choice, like us, and we felt they were kindred spirits. In the weeks following Michael's death I grew to understand just how much they cared about me.

In the aftermath of Michael's death some of the toughest things for me to deal with were administrative matters. Many of our affairs were not in joint names. So Clyth sat down and wrote a list of things I needed to do. We started with the booklet someone sent me from the Coroner's Office 'Information and Support Pack' for those bereaved by suicide.

The list was a long one:

1. Accountant – need to re-engage as Michael had sacked him six months before he died.
2. Australian Taxation Office – need a certified copy of the Death Certificate.
3. Commonwealth Bank – need yet another certified copy of the Death Certificate to close Michael's accounts and credit cards.
4. Australian Electoral Office – need another copy of the Death Certificate to delete Michael from the electoral roll.
5. Executor of Will – that was me.
6. Insurance:
   –Car insurance – cancel.
   –House insurance – change names.
7. Local Council – need yet another certified copy of the Death Certificate.
8. Titles Office – need Death Certificate.

There were also:

9. Medicare.
10. Superannuation fund.

11. Vehicle registration.
12. Sell Michael's car.
13. Utilities (gas, water, electricity, phone – needed Death Certificates as not all our affairs were in joint names).
14. Public library.
15. Lease out my vineyard at home.
16. Cancel vineyard lease at Eldridge Estate.

And the final insult:

17. Seek refund from Jetstar for trip Michael had booked for us to go to New Zealand – they needed even a Death Certificate to do this. We sent it to them. They were happy to refund my fare, but not Michael's. When I rang them, Jetstar told me they could not refund Michael's fare until they talked to him, as he had made the booking. They had to be kidding. I said I would like to talk to him too, but as you are looking at his Death Certificate, this is not possible. Fury was what I felt. I hung up the telephone and wrote Jetstar a letter. Finally the fare was refunded.

In all we had to obtain forty-two certified copies of the Death Certificate to change or amend my affairs. I was grateful my lawyer friend and neighbour Jenny Platt was at my side.

Many people regard me as an 'organisational queen' as I was always organising dinners and large parties. But these skills of mine were paralysed right at the time they were called upon. My friends kept asking me what they could do to help.

So Clyth wrote another list, this time the kind of help I needed around my property.

Things like:
1. BBQ buggered, gas bottle leaking.
2. Showerhead needs changing.
3. Power surge – oven and microwave need to be reset.
4. Gutters need cleaning.
5. Water tank maintenance.
6. Hug please.

The one escape I had from this administrative mess was playing bridge. At a time when everything around me seemed to be in chaos, it provided me with some structure and order. The only catch was that I kept running into people who were unaware that Michael had died and who asked after him. 'Has he been ill for long?' they asked. I was frank with my response. It was the only way to stop the questions.

So it was out with the booklet I received from the Coroner's Office again. I ran through the checklist of normal reactions to sudden loss. Physical: I was exhausted. Emotional: I was sad. Cognitive: I lacked concentration. Behavioural: disturbed sleep. Only four ticks – not too bad in the circumstances, as their grief checklist had twenty items.

One of the emotional items on the checklist was anger with the loved one who had taken his own life. But I wasn't.

I was relieved that his despair and pain were over. I had been the most important person in Michael's life, in part because he had a long history of falling out with so-called close male friends.

He fell out with a long-term university friend when we were considering buying a property from him. The friend failed to tell us that the property's road was subject to widening. Michael thought this was dishonest and severed their connection. Two other friends of his were discarded as he thought their work practices lacked rigour and he lost respect for them. He also fell out with others over differing political opinions. These episodes caused me angst because Michael withdrew and no longer wanted contact with these friends. It was difficult for me too as I was friends with their wives. Ultimately, he isolated himself and in the end confided in no one. Not even me.

My Empty Chair

In the years after Michael's death when I had guests for dinner I'd often set an extra place at the table, only to realise the chair would remain vacant. It was a habit that took a long time to break.

Michael was a great chef and we loved feeding our friends. I was his assistant and learned a great deal from him. My primary task was organising, making the table look inviting with colourful crockery, fine glasses, perfumed flowers from my garden, and indulging my obsession for beautiful serviettes.

After forty years of being partnered, setting the table as if I were still in a couple was not so much denial as habit. Our culture, its expectations, is geared for couples, not singles. My new role was underscored the first time I had to fill in a form describing my marital status as a widow. I ticked the box that defined me as a woman who has lost her husband by death.

Ever curious about words and their meanings, I searched the dictionary and found a much better definition of widow – as 'an extra hand dealt to the table in certain card games.' Players have a chance to use 'the widow' instead of their own hand. A bit like Michael and me. We were bridge partners for thirty years. Most life partners are unable to play as a team because they tend to criticise each other at the table. Remarkably, though, Michael and I played well together as a pair. We were both strategic thinkers and competitive.

Mind you, I did receive the odd lecture about what I should have done if he thought I had stuffed up. This was usually delivered at home after the event. Michael was brought up in a Catholic family and in these moments his righteousness often came to the fore. Most times I would listen and let it go. The bridge hand was already history, not worth arguing about. Arguing only fuelled Michael's critical side.

Someone gave me a card 'Marriages are just like bridge'. For the most part marriages are diamonds and hearts, but in the end they are clubs and a spade. For many decades our marriage was hearts and diamonds. It was only in the last phase of our partnership that clubs appeared and finally Michael chose a spade.

As Michael's mental health was disintegrating, he turned into a bully. It was like he was projecting his own pain onto me. He resented my wellness and sociability. He had become passively aggressive, not speaking to me or others if he thought we had done the wrong thing. Catching me smoking with friends, he would grab the cigarette from my mouth, much to the embarrassment of my friends and myself. He was becoming a different man from the one I had loved. Why would I put up with this stuff, I was asked. The answer was loyalty, not deserting a sinking soul.

Mental illness was painful, not only for him, but for those around him. I had tried my best.

Musical Memories

Six months after Michael had died I was home alone, on a midwinter's night. The fire was blazing and I was snuggled up on the couch with my cat Lily under my red woolly blanket.

My house was peaceful now. When Michael was alive there was always noise. His habit and his way was noise. The CD player was always on, along with radios blaring in his study and our bedroom. My grief felt noisy and my heart ached. For the first time in six months I decided music might be soothing. When I opened the CD player I discovered there were six CDs still in the machine, Roy Orbison, John Lennon, Bob Dylan, REM, Elvis Costello and Shane Howard. These must have been the songs Michael listened to on his final night.

Listening to the music on that wintery night was bone-cold lonely. I wanted to share the songs and memories with someone. I listened to those songs with a box of tissues beside me on the couch. I imagined a conversation with Luctus and tried to recall our favourite songs from the CDs.

Maybe Michael was listening to John Lennon singing 'Imagine'. The first time Michael and I heard this together was back in 1971 in our share house in Armadale. We both cried. It was a plea for hope. Or was it Lennon's untimely murder in 1980 he was thinking of? 'Imagine' is still my favourite song.

Bob Dylan was his favourite musician. We saw him perform every time he came to Australia. I remembered sitting in the rain at the Myer Music Bowl in 1975 as Dylan belted out 'Hard Rain'. The crowd were coated in raincoats and we loved bopping along with those lyrics even in the wet conditions. We also saw Dylan sing my favourite of his, 'Forever Young'. I used it at my young brother's funeral where I gave the eulogy. My brother was also a Dylan fan and we all went to those magic concerts together.

Michael and I both adored Roy Orbison. We saw him perform at the Palais Theatre three decades ago. 'Only the Lonely' was his standout song and listening to that song I could feel Michael's pain.

Michael's favourite band of all time was REM (Rapid Eye Movement) whom we saw perform in the States in 1992. It was exhilarating. Our most loved song was 'Everybody Hurts'. I imagine Michael was hurting because he was listening intently to the lyrics.

We both loved Australian musicians as well. We often went to see live bands in pubs, clubs and at music festivals. Each year we headed south to the Port Fairy Music Festival to hear our favourite musicians. People like Paul Kelly and Shane Howard from Goanna. In 1998 we settled into the marquee close to the stage. We knew Shane Howard would be performing. I wanted him to sing 'Solid Rock'. It was the last song in his bracket and the audience exploded with the power of the lyrics. We were all up dancing and cheering as he belted out those sentiments. It was so enlivening to be part of the crowd at this live performance.

For fifteen years Michael and I shared houses with friends

at Port Fairy. Our place was within walking distance of the footy ground where the festival was held. This allowed us to go home to eat and rest. We loved feeding friends, so our kitchen became our hub of activity. We all pitched in with the food frenzy. Our place was full of excitement as we listened to each other describing bands we had discovered.

Luctus, I want to read you something about love that I think is the truth. I got up from the couch and read some words from Helen Garner about the brutality of love. The lyrics of a thousand songs tell us you can't have love without pain.

Michael knew I would listen to the discs in the CD player. Maybe he wanted me to know his heartache and anguish on that last fateful night.

My Silhouette

After Michael's death I started feeling more like a silhouette than a fully embodied person. It was the hollowing out effect of grief that robbed me of my energy. The only things that provided comfort were words and books to escape my pain. It was last year, flicking through an art magazine, that I discovered an article about the origin of the word silhouette. Maybe time to share my findings with Luctus because silhouette seemed like my emotional state. Luctus was listening. Silhouette can be a noun or a verb. As a noun silhouette means delineation, form, outline, profile or shape. As a verb it means to etch or to stand out. It can be an active word to help me keep moving rather than standing still or being stuck.

Maybe the idea of etching in or delineating my silhouette could provide an opportunity to profile an authentic me. This might help me to make sense of my loss.

The origin of the word silhouette struck a chord with me. It starts with Étienne de Silhouette who was a French author and politician who lived from 1709 to 1767. He was described as the miserly finance minister in Louis XV's government. Given the political time, it looked like de Silhouette was 'taking from the rich to give to the poor' which is the name of a song by Marianne Faithful that always resonated with me. My social justice values and the idea of taking care of vulnerable people were appealing to me. I know this is a bit of a distraction. So be it. What is important to me is de Silhouette's hobby of cutting out paper shadow portraits of people. I gained a connection with Étienne de Silhouette when I pursued the art of decoupage.

Decoupage is a fine art form that originated in Italy in the 18th century. The word decoupage comes from the French word *découper* which means to cut out. It starts with cutting out paper images with special scissors. You carefully cut out the paper images from underneath so the edges of the cut outs are drawn down and disappear.

Luctus seemed a bit impatient because he could not work out why I spent hours and hours cutting out paper images and gluing them onto objects.

I decorate objects like urns, screens or ostrich eggs that tell a story about something I want to say. Design harmony with the piece of work is the key. I found a wonderful photocopy place that transforms my images into different sizes for me to work with. The paper images are then placed on the piece of work with Blu Tack until the design is right. The images are then carefully glued onto the piece. The next step is lacquering the object and after eight coats of lacquer the images are sanded back. In effect you are building up the painted background so the images are flat. A piece of decoupage usually has some forty coats of lacquer. It takes time to lacquer and sand, before the polishing begins. A finished piece of decoupage is smooth and shiny like porcelain.

My decoupage passion began in 1998 after I left full-time work, and continued for the next fifteen years. I'll give you an example of a piece of decoupage I created to help you understand the process better.

Once we were at a champagne tasting at The Point Restaurant on Albert Park Lake. There was a very beautiful wooden champagne box. In the middle of the box was a metal crest of the Moët & Chandon champagne house. We had all tasted the Cuvée Dom Pérignon Oenothèque vintage 1985. The director of the tasting said the box was available to the person who was able to answer one quiz question. 'What does Oenothèque mean?' he asked. Michael blurted out it meant 'wine library' so the box was ours. The box remained in my studio for two years before I found the images to cut out and decorate it with as a piece of decoupage. I discovered the images on two cards in the National Gallery in Canberra. The images were painted by Alphonse Mucha in 1899 for the Moët Champagne House as promotional posters for champagne. I could not believe my good fortune. One painting was 'Champagne White Star' and the second was called 'Reverie'. The central image in each card is typical of the Art Nouveau period. Mucha's characterisation of these Belle Époque maidens fashionably clad in jewelled headgear with immense sweeping skirts was perfect for my project. The images of pure and naive youthfulness personified the mood in Paris on the threshold of a new century. The design for my box was taking shape as both young female images were placed on either side of the metal Moët & Chandon crest. So an Art Noveau creation happened. I cut out and painted swirls in iridescent rich bronze to complement the autumnal colours of the female images. It took months to design before the coats of lacquer were applied, sanded and polished.

 Decoupage provided an outlet for my creativity. It was a joyful pastime and passion through the later difficult years living with depression because Michael would often stop taking his medication without telling me. I would only know because his eyes became dull and his mood would darken.

It made me feel helpless and frustrated because it took time for him to recover from depressive episodes and to get stabilised again on his antidepressant medication. He would be like a wet rag. In the ten years before Michael died, decoupage probably provided a distraction for me, some structure and direction.

It was no wonder before Michael's death you temporarily lost contact with your emotional cut-outs, and felt like a shadow portrait. It must have worn you down, wondering if it would ever end. It's not easy watching someone you loved disappearing from reach.

Together or Apart

Before Michael died, there had been very few nights in my life I'd spent alone in a house. I went from being with my parents to living with Michael for forty years. The only exceptions were the eight months when we separated in 1987 and the eleven days before he died in 2011. Both episodes were bewildering. Perhaps this is the way they happened.

During the first ten years of our marriage we had adult friends living with us. We owned a big house in St Kilda and friends who were between lovers or marriages came to stay. You never knew who would assemble for dinner. Michael was the cook until our dear friend Sue Picot came to live in our house. I met her on a bus in 1974 in Indonesia and discovered we were both studying social work at Monash University. When Sue arrived, she and Michael embarked on cooking competitions to find exotic dishes. Sue cooked spleen. It was of a deep red colour, lumpy looking meat, garnished with parsley. We had not eaten spleen before so I tackled the meat with my knife and fork. *Whoosh*, blood spurted into my face when I cut into the meat. We did not welcome spleen back to our dinner table again.

We had a warm welcoming place for strays and had lots of fun together. The highlight of the year in our big house was during the annual St Kilda Film Festival at the Palais Theatre. We opened our house as a soup kitchen for friends who had square eyes and needed a break and some sustenance.

There were 'walking wounded' women in our friendship circle. One weekend we were staying at a stray friend's beach house for the weekend. I had gone to bed early and the other three friends were still by the fire. The house was quiet. I woke to go to the toilet. Michael was not in our bed. I saw him fucking a recently separated friend in front of the fireplace. I exploded into tears.

Michael came to me. The affair scurried off. Michael and I went to our bedroom. I remember sitting in a foetal position in the big bay window beside our bed, rocking and crying. He did not have words to console me.

I could not understand why Michael would do this to me. What did I not notice? How long had this affair been going on? What an arsehole! I felt betrayed by him and her.

We talked and talked about trust, betrayal, opportunity and availability. Michael and I went to marriage guidance to get relationship help. I did forgive him in a way, but couldn't forget what I witnessed in front of the fire. I was to find out later from Michael that the affair lasted for six months in spite of his professed love for me. The reason he told me this was because the affair had dwindled.

Michael owned up to four affairs during our forty year marriage. They seemed to happen about every seven years… a seven year bitch and itch… someone said. Each affair caused me angst and pain. I began wondering if men are wired differently to women. Pity we like men so much. How did I feel about these affairs? They felt like shards in my heart. The affair pattern continued because cruelly each had spent a generous amount of time at our place getting support.

Michael always reassured me these affairs meant little to him. They were just 'flings'. It was the 'fling' in 1987 that finally led to our amicable separation. It seemed Michael was not wired for mutual fidelity and I'd had enough.

The affair was with my brother's ex whom Michael had helped with financial planning after she split up with my young brother. At this time in 1987 Michael wanted to move to the country to grow grapes. I was at the height of my career in Corrections in Melbourne. Maybe we still loved each other, but we were going in different directions. His infidelity was too much for me. We sold our property and settled our affairs without lawyers. We were still friends but went our separate ways.

Michael bought an apple orchard in central Victoria near where the affair lived. I sought the help of an accountant friend to buy an apartment in South Yarra. I felt alone making this decision. On reflection it makes sense now because Michael and I had married when we were young and always made decisions together, be it about property or how we wanted to live our life together.

I struggled living alone, missing the intimacy and companionship we had shared. My aloneness was painful. All that missing and wanting and not finding the love and kindness I craved. It took Michael two months to realise he couldn't live without me and he came begging for my forgiveness. Michael had split up with his affair and was to sell his country property. I listened intently to his story about what had not worked out for him. It did not surprise me that the affair thought he was a control freak and she did not understand him. I was wary of his approach after the heartache and pain we had caused each other.

He started inviting me out to dinner. I did not go.

Michael asked if I would join the Thursday nighters' tennis group as an emergency. This turned out to be weekly tennis nights. Michael kept ringing and calling around. Michael did the music for a big party I was giving. He was not invited. Michael soon told me he had another partner; her name was 'clinical depression'. Aah!!! Beware, I was feeling ambivalent. Love is a risky business and with his track record I wondered. Loyalty or betrayal could be on the cards.

Michael's wooing of me continued and he came around to my place to do 'boy jobs', changing washers on leaky taps and helping me with my computer.

I relented after three months and went out to dinner with him. Michael bought me a Diane Freis dress from Georges, the 'exclusive' shop in Collins Street.

We started seeing each other again. Michael fell in love with my new cat, Eartha. She was a rescue cat, totally black and psychotic. Eartha ripped the curtains and my stockings regularly. Michael probably identified with her madness. He built a ladder system so Eartha could go to the Bridge Club next door when I was not at home. Long hours at my workplace dealing with suicides, assaults and mayhem gave Michael the opportunity to bond with Eartha in the garden.

The dinner invitations involved every night I wasn't working. We did love each other. Michael moved into my apartment eight months after we had separated. Our connections felt fragile but we were on the same path again. We agreed to be kinder and care for each other this time.

We were together again but his clinical depression came with him.

Respite

Living with Michael and his demons became more difficult as the years progressed. The side effects of the antidepressant medication made him feel foggy in his brain. He would just stop taking his pills and spiral down. It was in 2005 that total despair hit him. He was voluntarily admitted to the psychiatric ward at The Alfred Hospital. Michael told me he was thinking about methods of killing himself. He raved on to me about how useless he felt and that he did not deserve me. I visited him at the hospital each day, taking him treats. We used to walk around Fawkner Park and he would tell me about the bizarre things that happened in the hospital. Other patients were slashing up with razor blades and their behaviour made him feel well. Michael went back on his medication and regained his equilibrium, and came home after three weeks.

His despairing episodes came and went. Although Michael could not ask for help, he bullied me into accepting I needed help to curb my drinking habits. 2007 was a particularly stressful year. We had demolished our house in Red Hill and we were building a new one. Moving into rented premises was disruptive and all Michael could do was lie on the couch. He did not move one box. I was exhausted and exasperated. My coping mechanism became alcohol. I was drowning out my pain with booze because I found watching him disintegrate stressful.

Michael and I had always been big drinkers and enjoyed wine. However, because of the medication he would spend days in bed recovering after a big night.

Michael resented my ability to get up early and go walking with friends, which is always a good start to my day. I was drinking too much and this was obvious to close friends who talked to me about their concerns. Some would say I have a larrikin streak which most of the time I could get away with. Not now. I was finding self-destructive behaviour was not a helpful way to cope.

I became an in-patient at the Beleura Hospital alcohol program. It was respite from caring for Michael. It was a relief to reflect and rest. I was discovering my care threshold for other people's woes. The program was run from a rural property in Mornington where patients could relax in the garden after our therapeutic sessions. One colourful character I met explained how he disguised his alcohol abuse from his wife by being in his shed. He would drink vodka because it did not smell on his breath. The camouflage was complete because he put petrol on his hands, pretending he was working with lawnmowers.

I was pleased to learn there was no physical damage because of my drinking history. The staff considered that with my stable background, employment record and social history I might succeed with a controlled drinking approach.

The program was helpful because it was time away from routines and caring for Michael. I had been at Beleura Hospital for two weeks when Michael took me to see his dying mother. She wanted to see me. I always loved his mother's pioneering spirit. Granny, as we called her, came to stay at Red Hill each week after her husband died. Granny died a few days later.

Michael had a very close relationship with his mother and her death had a profound effect on him because he struggled with his grief. I did not return to Beleura because Michael wanted my emotional support at this difficult time. We went home to cuddle and snuggle each other. We called them 'cuddles from behind', lying entwined in the warmth of our bed or in front of the fire. Many tissues came and went. Revealing vulnerability and owning up to imperfections and accepting them was starting to make sense to me.

It was not until after Michael died that I discovered he had provided respite for me in everyday living. Now on my own, I became frustrated by my ineptness about mechanical things. I am living in the country with septic tanks, water tanks, power outages and water pumps. It is pathetic that I do not understand or want to know how all the systems work. It is worse with anything digital – computer, DVD machine and Telstra.

It was a year after Michael died that an unannounced tradesman arrived at my place. The doorbell was ringing and someone was banging on the door. No one was there when I opened it.

The next thing I found was a tradesman on my back deck. He was yelling at me about my fucking doorbell not working. He told me he was here to pump out my sewage pit and demanded to know where it was. Stay calm, I told myself, because my prison experience taught me it was unwise to handle aggression with aggression. Who was this 'poo' rodent?

I took a few deep breaths before explaining to him that

people do not come to my house without a name, without an appointment and without me knowing what they are here for. The 'poo' rodent began back-pedalling down the steps and he finally shouted his name and apologised. Off he scurried. I complained to my sewage contractor, who had sent the 'poo' rodent without consulting me. Why do such incidents upset me so much? Probably because it is an intrusion into my privacy. Also safety and security is paramount to me and probably to other women not used to living alone.

Michael, before he died, had spared me the dealing with 'poo' rodents. Respite.

Awareness of my limitations, understanding what frustrates me and learning how to deal with everyday mechanical things were things that required my problem-solving skills. Put it on the 'to do' list. Time to grow up and problem-solve by myself instead of being stuck in my learned helplessness state. I still ask or pay for help.

Seeking Help

Six months after Michael died I was stuck. Grief, grief, please go away. I visited my doctor who recommended I get some professional help from a psychologist.

The therapist was dressed in purple and green garb. She had a head full of long red curly hair. I was coated in red clothes, and my red felted wool strawberry hat made her smile. We both laughed when we looked at each other. My first impression was of a zany, colourful character. Our interaction was likely to be feisty. Empathy oozed from the beginning session.

Getting to know myself felt like a daunting task. Too close, too personal, exposure, wondering. How would I cope with someone exploring me? Was this why Michael avoided seeking 'real help'?

The most useful task the therapist gave me was to write a diary for the next six months. This took the form of answering three questions: What am I grateful for? What makes my heart sing and brings me joy? How do I feel emotionally?

The most consistent entry about what I was grateful for was the support and love I received from and gave my friends. This was followed by good health, intelligence and my curiosity. My garden was what made my heart sing. Nine months after Michael died I created my whimsical herb and rose garden with the help of my friend Wendy.

We designed the shape that complemented my favourite sculptural jacaranda tree. We transplanted the roses from our vineyard at Eldridge Estate. The highly perfumed deep red roses called Mr Lincoln were my favourite. They came from our pinot noir rows. Next were the Just Joeys which are salmon coloured and came from our sauvignon blanc rows. Finally, the Peter Frankenfeld which are a deep pink fragrant rose from the gamay rows. The colours of the roses matched the colours of the grapes.

People always ask me why roses are planted at the ends of rows of vines. Originally this was because if aphids were attacking the roses, it was likely they would attack the grapes. They were like canaries down a mine shaft. There are now other ways to protect the grapes and roses in the vineyard are now decorative.

Next came the herb planting. Seven different aromatic basil plants, sage, rosemary, parsley and mint. The final touch to the garden was when I built a woven seat around the base of the jacaranda tree, made out of vine trunks and canes.

When I began the diary I felt empty, because I had lost touch with my emotions. But slowly and gradually my moods improved. It was difficult to write about my 'inside' self. Putting myself back together again I visualised as etching in my silhouette.

I was trying to let the pain out. I was trying to be honest with myself. My therapist suggested listening to my intuition as it might help me gain insight into my spiritual and emotional self. She asked me to describe my spiritual self.

This is what I wrote…

My spirituality is my unique essence which has been

shaped by my family of origin, experiences, intellectual heritage and my choices in work, love and life. It is about how I think, feel and approach life and its challenges. My spirituality provides the balance and harmony and my grief has been an opportunity to learn and grow.

My most important values arise from my commitment to social justice – honesty, integrity, fairness and compassion in both work and play. Elisabeth Kübler-Ross, who was a gutsy woman on an inspirational life journey, makes the point about the importance of unconditional love, not only of others, but ourselves, and not being constrained by conventions.

I express and seek my spirituality through the love I give and receive in the community in which I live, from my friends and family and my creative attachment to my environment – soil for growing my whimsical garden and my vineyard.

Sometimes I sound so distant and formal with my words. Is this because of the work I did? Or is it a way to protect myself?

Both probably. My therapist suggested I needed to focus on what makes me happy rather than people pleasing. Seeking help gave space for me. I continued with my diary and read everything the therapist suggested. At our last session, she said to me, 'Piss off, you are weller than me.' It felt like I was given an elephant stamp and permission to begin my new life. Where do I want to be in two years' time? What did I want to do? The therapist taught me to identify my strengths and capacities and to build on them. Emotional growth was the clear goal. She did start me thinking and feeling about what it would be like to be partnered again, whatever form that might take.

The therapy gave me confidence to go exploring again.

I went off to the Byron Bay Writers' Festival at the end of therapy. I attended a session with sexual anthropologists on love and romance.

I discovered the term 'limerence'. I was intrigued to learn it is the enchanted period of early love when sex is elevated to the realms of the divine when sexual desire peaks. The anthropologist explained this is because you are getting to know your partner and dopamine and testosterone are surging through your bodies. For me, now a 'widow' who had been married for forty years, the chemistry of couples was forefront in my mind. Curious me.

At the Writers' Festival, during this session, another speaker gave her research findings of a survey of three thousand couples in the United Kingdom. Apparently romance between couples lasted two years, six months and twenty-five days into marriage.

As part of this session there were discussions about the EL James trilogy of *Fifty Shades of Grey*. Who had read them? It was interesting to hear from others who thought the books were politically incorrect trash centring around lust. I disagreed. To me the books were about redemption and the power a person has to heal by summoning up enough courage to act from the heart. I thought how differently we interpret stuff.

Couple Envy

Fresh from the Byron Bay Writers' Festival in 2015 I landed in Hong Kong to stay with a couple who are friends from Red Hill. They had lived in Hong Kong for decades and belonged to prestigious clubs. We were booked for dinner at the China Club. It has a famous restaurant set amongst a huge collection of contemporary paintings. The walls were panelled in wood and the tables were set with bone china and luxurious red serviettes. There were also private leather booths near our table.

From where I was sitting I watched and observed a couple in a seemingly private booth. They looked like lovers. He was an older Caucasian man dressed in a tailored suit. She was a much younger Chinese woman in a slinky black dress, sparkling diamond necklace and rings. They only had eyes for each other and did not appear to notice me watching their interaction. Clandestine, furtive but knowing touches. Yearning in anticipation of caresses and coupling. Bubbles were dancing in their champagne flutes and I watched them clinking their glasses. Smiling faces told me they were celebrating something, maybe an anniversary of their meeting. He touched her hand so lovingly and then they clasped each other's fingers. Their hands were a perfect fit, like gloves. Their eyes sparkled. They were glowing and enjoying their love for each other. This couple were not taking photos.

The next day my friends took me to the palatial Peninsula Hotel where couples go to celebrate. It was afternoon tea time. I watched another couple, this time young, in action. Shiny new wedding rings were being photographed. I stared as they melted into each other. The champagne cork had popped and bubbles of delight were also in the eyes of the honeymooners. A waiter brought out a silver cake stand in the shape of the Eiffel Tower to their table. It was covered in colourful exotic little cakes which they delicately ate. What desire they had for each other. I was pleased for their joy. More photos, which were being sent to their loved ones.

Watching this couple reminded me of the time Michael and I bought a bottle of Perrier-Jouët Belle Époque champagne. We went to Paris for our 20th wedding anniversary. Michael had bought us the matching champagne flutes that were hand-painted with the signature Belle Époque rose. This was a happy occasion and we celebrated our love in style. It is still my favourite champagne and I treasure my gift of the flutes.

It is such fun trying to imagine how and why couples meet and become connected. Is it about chemistry or availability, I wondered. Observing these couples set me thinking that love is really about care and kindness in whatever forms that takes. Oh to be truly loved again was becoming my mantra. Could I possibly fall in love again at my age? I wished for more insight and was bewildered and at sea about the prospect.

Was I just succumbing to the romantic ideal that my resurrection would be due to meeting a wonderful man who could rescue me? Time to talk to Luctus.

Our society is geared towards couples and most people

enjoy the companionship and intimacy that blossoms in loving relationships. Great writers tell us this. Helen Garner observed nobody can imagine anything more terrible than being solitary. The wisdom of Marilyn French strikes a chord too. She makes the point that loneliness is not longing for company, it is a longing for kind.

Being separated with the prospect of divorce felt different from being single by suicide. The core difference related to choice and how I and others perceived those choices. Survivor of our marriage, feeling no guilt and believing in my heart I tried my best. I was engulfed by sadness that Michael and I were not able to enjoy what should have been the best time in our lives, our retirement years.

In my profession I had learned that when a person makes a decision to suicide, they are often relieved, feel calmer and do not talk about it. Maybe this is what happened with Michael as our last friend he had dinner with, Carolyn, reported he was calm. It is the finality of suicide that echoes and the realisation that now it is only through memories that a loved one continues to live on.

I wondered how the honeymooners from the Peninsula Hotel and the lovers from the China Club were faring together. I had watched these couples in the limerence phase of love when the pheromones were flying. But Alain de Botton suggests in his book *The Course of Love* that this is only the beginning. It is the course of love that needs working on if love is to endure. Love is a skill.

Restless

It was two years since Michael had died and I wondered if Luctus could help me to understand why I was so restless.

You need more rest and sleep to help you heal. You go out too much in search of something. Find things that soothe you.

It is reading and words that I find most soothing. I can escape into books. They are my companions.

Well, keep reading. You have taken positive steps through regular walking, pilates and exercise. Build on them.

But if I don't go out, I won't meet the man of my dreams.

You are in no fit state to take up emotionally with anyone. Inner calm before any other liaison in your life might be better. Grief is painful and it is an individual journey. It will take time to reclaim your former energy levels which have been temporarily stolen by grief. Michael's death was an event at the end of a process. You had both been grieving for years because of his depression. There is no prescribed way or set amount of time in dealing with loss. How an individual reacts to events is important because it is something an individual can influence. Significant loss remains but one can learn to move through it, partner it and take action to use it creatively to find out a purpose in one's life.

How much time? I'm impatient and alone. It is awful. I can't get used to it.

Think about other things that cheer you up. Music, curling up in bed with Lily or cooking. Name the soothing bits and enjoy the experience.

I'm finding cooking is soothing. I've been making Michael's signature dishes to share with friends. They kind of connect me to him.

It is not really cooking, but I love making gravlax. Michael taught me how. You buy 800 grams of raw Atlantic salmon and cure it in a mixture of salt flakes, caster sugar, dill and a dash of vodka. You tightly wrap the fish in the mixture. Refrigerate and tip off liquid every eight hours. It takes forty hours, voila! It cures itself. I often take gravlax to drinks on Sunday night at Main Ridge Estate. The sauce is mustard and dill. I serve it on little rounds of pumpernickel bread.

Sounds delicious. Perfect idea, something soothing for you and it also meets your need to show care and kindness for others. Fill the void with distractions, let yourself cry, listen to music at home, watch programs on iview at your leisure. Stop running around in circles.

It's hard. I've always been a bit hyperactive, packing into a day what normal people do in a week. I once tried to be ordinary, but never got the hang of it.

You are not normal. You like being different. Look at the clothes you wear. They make a statement about your colourful and playful personality. You surround yourself with zany items in your house. Who else puts hydrangeas in the bottom of glass vases to camouflage the stalks of flower stems? You are creative. Please keep doing stuff like that. It helps you to get accolades, doesn't it? I think you seek approval from others.

I love your melting eyes and luscious lips because you

are watching over me. Dear Luctus, you are so kind and wise. I wish you were here in the flesh.

Compounding Grief

After Michael's death I began looking through my journals and diaries to bring back memories of good things we shared, when we both felt emotionally connected. I wrote a short story called 'Travel Traumas & Triumphs' which brought a smile to my face. I wondered about reading this to my brother, Geoff, who was coming to lunch. It was a sunny day and I set the table for us out on the deck so we could enjoy the garden too. This is a place of solace for me where I often sit and read. Maybe Luctus could join us.

It was a milestone for us. It was the 20th anniversary of the death of our young brother Rob and the 10th anniversary of Dad's death. Geoff had rung to see if I wanted to go with him to visit the family plot at the Springvale Crematorium to mark the occasion. I could not go, because my memories of being there before were too painful.

Clonk, clonk – Mum's and Kay's coffins had disappeared behind the curtain and were dropped down into the fireplace for their cremations. They were gone and would now be ashes. I never want my ashes in a box; I'm too much of a free spirit myself to be so confined.

My family tree is deciduous. Why the leaves fell into a compost of sorrow was because two of my siblings died young. I am always happy to see my brother as we are the only survivors from our family. We have a shared history and did some daring things together.

One adventure found us on television when I was eighteen years of age. We appeared on a television program called 'Blind Date'. Geoff had seen an advertisement in the newspaper, calling for volunteers. He made an appointment and we rocked up to the television studio to be instructed by the producers. I was part of a panel of three young women. The program was a direct telecast. The so-called male prize was behind a screen so he could not see us. We all had to answer the same questions and the potential blind date chose the answer he liked best. The woman who scored highest won the prize. Each of us women had to describe ourselves in two words. 'Sweet and innocent' was my clichéd response. But I was not a winner. Naming a flaw of mine as 'impatience' did not do the trick either. I did score a point for my favourite comedian who was Peter Sellers. So it went on like this for about twelve questions. You will not be surprised that I missed out on the blind date, who turned out to be Molly Meldrum of rock celebrity fame. My debut television appearance was to be my last.

I recall another event when I was eight years old. Geoff was chanting 'Father, Uncle, Cousin, King' to me. I did have a father, an uncle and a cousin, but not a king. I wondered if he was trying to describe our family tree or teaching me to swear. My mother was cross with Geoff and told me it was a rude word, which we were not to use.

You sound happy when you tell these tales because you are connected to your brother. Your shared history is special and important to savour.

I was pleased to see Geoff and we went for a garden tour

before lunch. My herbs and roses were all blooming and he laughed again when he saw my red tree. Geoff talked about the roses in the family plot at the Crematorium and how sad it made him feel. He then started talking about his traumatic memories of our sister Kay who had died fifty years ago.

Luctus and I were listening carefully to Geoff's outpourings about how angry he was for a decade about the circumstances surrounding her treatment and care. Kay was eighteen and Geoff was twenty when they were batching at home together at the family house. Our parents had taken my brother and me on a beach holiday at Anglesea. There were no phones at the beach house, before the days of mobile phones. It was late afternoon when a policeman turned up at the house with the bad bad news. Kay was critically ill in hospital and we urgently needed to return to Melbourne.

It was some time before we managed to hear the saga and what Geoff had dealt with. Kay had headaches and visited the doctor a few times, but he had just sent her off to have her eyes tested. The headaches continued and Geoff was so worried and frustrated he had taken her to a hospital emergency department. The doctors discovered she had an aneurysm – a brain haemorrhage. Mum and Dad raced to the hospital to see her, but it was not long before another aneurysm took her away from us. My recollection of the event was that she disappeared without real warning. It made no sense and seemed so unfair. We were all in shock.

Kay's beautiful titian red hair was shaved off during the operations they did to save her life. I still treasure her ponytail and it is kept in a leather box. Her hair colour is still vivid after fifty years and I imagine it smells of her. Kay was a year older than me and we shared a bedroom until she died. We called each other 'legs' because we often slept in the same bed together.

Geoff was angry and tissues were out because of our loss. The suddenness. The lunch with Geoff, talking about Kay, unravelled again what I thought was settled fifty years ago. I wondered why we had not had this conversation before.

We cried together. My grief about my sister came swimming back. The sudden disappearance of Michael from my life seemed to compound the grief. I cried as I read a story to my brother about the travelling traumas and triumphs Michael and I shared.

After the lunch with my brother and after reading Emily Bitto's book *The Strays*, I wrote my first poem about my sister. Bitto coined the term 'leg sister' in her novel. Kay was my blood sister and 'leg sister'.

LEG SISTERS

Here's the thing about aloneness
It is painful but can be soothed
It is a long lonesome journey but grief
Can change colour and soften into sorrow
I didn't always feel alone
Loss in my life allowed it to creep in
The first time I felt its grip was
When my sister Kay disappeared
An aneurysm
Took her away
Suddenly life took a new turn for those who were left
I had lost my leg sister.

Deep connection sleeping tangled up together
Skin to skin, heart to heart, trust and safety

SILHOUETTE OF SORROW

Like a trial chaste marriage
So when Kay disappeared it was suddenly like I was
Alone in that bed. The world is a bed
Our shared secrets had nowhere to go.

I picked myself up I suppose you could say
Or at least I felt I did as my mother was heartbroken
And needed my help
I filled the aloneness with
Supporting my parents: a purpose outside of myself.

How did I soothe myself?
I buried myself with my close friends
Sought connections, heart to heart, life to life
I was fortunate to have another leg sister
She called and I went to her place
That night we slept in her bed all tangled up together.

A female friend is a wondrous thing
Always there to listen and share
I have always had my friends in my life
I find and nurture them and
My kindness and care bind us in friendship.
If aloneness was a colour, it would be black
If hurting was a colour it would be red
If soothing was a colour it would be yellow.

Aloneness has come to me again and again
Loss, grief and sorrow are part of my silhouette
I have seen and touched the blacks and reds
I feel bruised by the reds, just like a wound.

Is grief the price you pay for love?
Is sadness and sorrow the price you pay for loss of love?
Sorrow feels like the scar and it will always be with me
Sorrow lives in a pocket in my body
and I pat her, touch her
Talk to her. Sometimes I hold my heart at the same time.

I have put the poem in the leather box with Kay's ponytail. She would like that.

After my sister died the red clothing of my youth turned black. Did this symbolise my aloneness? Was I in mourning?

I remember my mother begging me not to get married in a black outfit. I compromised. The year was 1972 and she made my wedding dress. The material was luminous pink, red and purple swirls with a silk hood. I wear it now to '70s' dress-up parties.

I was still in black clothing until my friend Amanda convinced me to go with her to a seminar called 'Colour Me Beautiful' – a slick operation where you get your colours done. The colour swatch system had four seasons. The theory was to wear clothes that match your complexion and hair colour. We were told people will compliment you on your appearance if you are colour matched and you will feel lighter and happier.

I was picked from the crowd to illustrate the system because I was blonde, wearing black. As I sat on that stage under bright lights they told me I looked old and sad. I was a Spring and should wear red and cobalt blue. These were my colours. I came alive again and reclaimed my red clothes after a decade in black. The system works and people always compliment me on my appearance if I wear my colours.

Vulnerability

Four years after Michael died, I discovered the work of Dr Brené Brown on the power of vulnerability on a 'TED Talks' TV program. Her groundbreaking research challenges everything we think we know about vulnerability and dispels the widely accepted myth that it's a weakness. She argues that it is in fact a strength, and when we shut ourselves off from revealing our true selves, we grow distanced from the things that bring purpose and meaning to our lives.

Ever curious about words and their meanings, I searched the dictionary and found the word vulnerability comes from the Latin word *vulnerare* meaning 'to wound'. Brené Brown has redefined vulnerability as 'uncertainty, risk and emotional exposure'. From a decade of research she learned that vulnerability is the cradle of emotional experience we all crave. It is also the birthplace of love, belonging, joy, courage, empathy and creativity.

I wondered what Michael would say about the word vulnerability. My guess is he would have gone with the dictionary definition. He felt wounded. Michael would have been unable to say it means asking for help, asking for forgiveness or admitting he was afraid and imperfect. This is probably why he never really sought help because he wanted to be protected against emotional exposure.

On the other hand, because Michael was an intellectual

he would have identified with her analysis. Michael had admitted to me he felt unworthy, guilty about his infidelity, disconnected, joyless, and lacking energy and a purpose and meaning in his life – which are some of the items on Brown's checklist. Michael was unable to share these descriptors with friends or professionals. His vulnerability seemed to lead to his isolation.

Professor Brown poses two key questions that are at the heart of the matter: How do we learn to embrace our vulnerabilities and imperfections so that we can be engaged in our lives from a place of authenticity and worthiness? And how do we cultivate the courage, compassion and connection that we need to recognise that we are enough – that we are worthy of love, belonging and joy?

Fierce questions to wonder about and try to find answers to. Her insights might provide a new way of beginning to understand what happened.

I didn't feel unworthy which might be a start in answering Brown's questions.

The Last Year

Brown's research was the trigger for me to try to piece together the last year of my life with Michael. Although it was four years after his death, I was still wondering what else I could have done or should have seen.

I woke at 6 am on 7 March 2011 to find Michael was not in our bed. Where could he be? I searched the house and came out to the living room to find a letter on the bench. It was from him. A suicide note. Instructions for me about our financial affairs. 'Sorry', it said. I was bewildered and just stared at the note trying to make sense of it. What had I missed?

Some minutes later I heard a car and a bang so raced to open the front door.

There was a bedraggled Michael dragging a doona. His eyes were glazed and he was unsteady on his feet. Michael's speech was slurred as he tried to explain.

I gave him a hug, shuddering in shock. 'Let me take you to hospital, what's going on?'

'Nup, I just need to sleep. I took twenty valium pills and thought the gas bottle in our stainless steel vat would be enough. But I failed. I always fail you. I am never enough. The pills made me sick.'

He refused to go to hospital and asked me not to tell anyone. Michael collapsed into bed. I wondered about calling an ambulance. A quandary of care or respecting his wishes. I watched over him. He slept, slept and slept.

When he finally came to, I gave him breakfast in bed, always our ritual. I was listening to his jumbled pain. Depression seemed like a rerun of a film he was stuck in that he didn't know how to share. It seemed he was in a struggle with himself, trying to deal with the guilt and shame in his past. All those bashings and demeaning insults he experienced at his Catholic boarding school were part of his dark side. I encouraged him to see his psychiatrist. He was clearly distressed but rejected help.

A few days later we were playing together in a social tennis day, something that had always connected us. We were doing well. He seemed OK until he ruptured his Achilles tendon at the tennis net. I took him to Rosebud Hospital where we waited and waited. He looked forlorn and dispirited. I held his hand. He needed to go to Frankston Hospital for surgery. What upset him more than anything else was not being able to tend his vines. He was frustrated because it was leaf plucking time to expose the grapes to the dappled sun.

I did the work with friends as my helpers. Michael wanted to be part of the action and insisted on me driving the tractor with him on a chair in the trailer. He wanted to monitor the vineyard for mildew.

I was scared about our safety because my tractor skills are not my forte. He should have been resting but he was restless. I was physically exhausted from the vineyard work – leaf plucking and trying to get the birds out from under the nets every day. A nightmare. Michael seemed calmer over the next week because he approved of our efforts in the vineyard and he was healing after surgery.

A month later he was in the Oncology Ward at Peter MacCallum Hospital having a melanoma removed. Between tending the vines and visiting him every day I was strung out emotionally and physically.

An old friend, Helen Owens, came to visit Michael at Peter MacCallum Hospital. She brought Michael a gift. It was a novel, *A Sense of an Ending* by Julian Barnes. Helen had endured breast cancer treatment for fifteen years. Her attitude to chemotherapy, radiation and trials was positive even though she watched her peers die one by one. Helen remarked we might think it was a strange book to give a friend in an oncology ward. I read the book to Michael during his hospital stay. Tears came flooding. I can now see the parallels with Michael and the protagonist in this novel because they both struggled with their inner selves, risk and uncertainty.

Recovering at home after his operation Michael tried to be in his beloved vineyard. He got lymphoedema. Michael was told gangrene and amputation of his leg would result without complete rest. He was totally frustrated and despairing.

The 2011 grape vintage was problematic because of the mildew on the grapes. Michael was having his own inner mildew. He toiled on emotionally and physically. At vintage, when the grapes are picked, he was in a wheelchair directing operations.

Our friends enabled vintage to happen. Without them I could not have survived. Michael, by this time, was in a total state of disrepair. At home he was brooding, joyless and grumpy. He did brighten up planning the menu for the annual dinner we hosted at Bernard's Restaurant in Balnarring to share our wines and thank our helpers –

always the culmination of a year of hard work tending grapes and finally picking them. Michael gave a speech and thanked all the friends who had helped us through this very difficult year.

After Michael's speech a number of friends insisted on him acknowledging my role in that vintage. They talked about how wonderful I had been with my team of helpers, which made him angry. The next morning he went berserk and told me he wanted a divorce because he could not stand the accolades I received when he had spent eleven years hard at work with the wines. Everybody loved me, not him, he said. I tried to console him, but he was not listening anymore.

He wanted me to obtain independent financial advice and get agents to value our property for the divorce. I did both things and he thought the advice I was given was wrong. He was being the righteous altered Michael who was clearly unwell. I was still living with him at home until he had the locks changed – shutting me out. My friends were becoming increasingly concerned for my safety. They knew he had a gun. I was beginning to feel unsafe myself.

On 1 December 2011 I became a 'refugee' from my own home, staying with friends in Melbourne and Red Hill. He died on 13 December 2011. During those harrowing two weeks, I spoke to him most days. One night he told me he had sold half of our share portfolio. He told me he did not know why he did this.

What to do about the shares? I was grateful to be surrounded by supportive friends who provided wise counsel. I then went into action and was amazed I could cancel all our accounts on that night. This upset Michael. He was also desperate to see me, because he wanted me to sign papers about our superannuation fund. Michael also needed my signature to complete the transaction of selling the shares.

Six months earlier he had sacked our accountant, whom he had fallen out with. He was looking for me in Red Hill. He was resisting help from our GP, whom I talked to. Michael was on a mission.

My lawyer advised against seeing him or signing papers. She spoke to his solicitor about agreeing on a process to resolve matters and her concerns about the gun and my safety. His lawyer was to ask him to hand in his gun to the police. Michael did not return his calls and no one had spoken to him in the past twenty-four hours.

It was a Tuesday and I felt in my bones that all was not well. I asked a friend to call in to visit our house. He was anxious and did not go in or get too close as he was out of his comfort zone. He came back to where I was staying and said Michael did not look well. He asked if I have keys to the house. My friend Helen Davison then took charge. She went to our place to find the door was open. Michael was dead with the gun in his lap. I had tried my best over the last harrowing year but he had pushed me away.

What do I do next? I did not want to think about it, I just needed to sleep. There is something safe about sleep – what is that about? Is it blocking out the pain or is it part of grieving? Is it about looking for safety? It was new to me and caused me discomfort. I was in total shock. Michael was gone from me.

I did not know his road to a gun until I received the Coroner's Report on 13/10/14.

- December 1, 2010 – application to Victoria Police to obtain a firearms licence.

- January 5, 2011 – licence granted.
- February 24, 2011 – gun purchased.
- March 22, 2011 – gun registered.

A Plea

Nearly three years after Michael's death I received a call from the Coroner's Office, informing me the Coroner had completed her investigation and made a finding without an inquest.

The three year time delay had occurred because I had given permission for Michael's case to be included in a study dealing with mental illness and the firearms licensing process.

I had faith lessons could be learned.

The Coroner's Registrar explained it might be upsetting for me to read the details of Michael's death in a formal report. She suggested that perhaps I could read it with a friend.

How caring they were. I was impressed by their approach.

The report arrived in the post and I looked carefully at the envelope for a while and then decided not to read it, yet.

I grabbed the box of tissues. What did I fear would be in the report? What did I do? Instead I gave the report to my favourite niece, Kriss Will. She was my filter, my emotional protector.

Kriss read the report and told me there was nothing

new about the facts. She thought that I would be interested to know guidelines were being developed for health professionals dealing with the firearms licensing process.

I was relieved to hear this was happening because there were complex moral and medical confidentiality issues at stake.

It is only recently that I have been brave enough to read the Coroner's Report.

I was anxious and dreaded reading about this tragic event which was so painfully personal.

Sure enough, the Coroner's Report about Michael's death was clothed in bureaucratic language. Formal, distant and clinical.

It reminded me of the suicide audits that were prepared when a prisoner died in custody. These were commissioned by the Corrections Health Board in an attempt to assemble all the facts of a tragic death of a prisoner. The Office of Corrections and the Health Department had a 'duty of care' to keep prisoners safe and secure. These audits were a way of testing how well 'our duty of care' was exercised. They often provided useful insights about procedures that needed to change. As I scanned the Coroner's Report, those same professional eyes of mine were looking for clues in Michael's history. But this time it was personal.

I was wondering if an examined death is as important as an examined life. Could or should I have done anything differently? In a way it was an audit of my actions. It felt like it was a test of my emotional stamina as well. The box of tissues was handy.

I was very surprised to read Michael had told his

psychiatrist that his depressive episodes began in 1984 following a car accident. There was no accident.

Why would Michael have made this up? Maybe he was looking for a physical trigger to explain his mental illness to himself.

The Coroner's Report contained thirty-five paragraphs outlining the circumstances that led to Michael's suicide.

Michael would have chipped in about the number thirty-five. His probing mathematical brain would have made up an equation or an irreverent poem about summing up his life in this way. My tears wet the pages. I pressed on reading about an aspect of Michael's life. He had been a larger than life character to me.

What were the Coroner's findings pursuant to Section 67 [2], **Coroner's Act 2008**?

She found Michael 'died from a self-inflicted gunshot injury to the head in circumstances where he intended to end his own life.'

Those formal words kept echoing in my ears for days. So final. So clinical. I was relieved that the Coroner did not say he 'committed' suicide.

What else had the Coroner found?

She found the death of Michael highlights the problems associated with the mechanism of self-reporting mental illness when applying for a firearms licence. Michael had shown me the application form he had to fill in to apply for a gun licence.

He thought the form was a joke. 'What if I do not tell Victoria Police about my depression? How would they know? I could just lie.' This comment should have been warning bells for me.

I suggested he seek a supporting letter from his psychiatrist if he had to proceed with the gun licence.
    I heard manipulative Michael talking to his psychiatrist about a supporting letter. He wanted me to hear this conversation.

The Coroner noted Michael did seek a letter from his psychiatrist.
    I read the evidence the psychiatrist gave to the Coroner. My blood was boiling. I was so angry as I reread it.

The psychiatrist had never before had such a request in his professional work. He was unfamiliar with the police and licensing procedure in this area of the law. He was cautious about facilitating the accessing of a firearm by an individual with a well documented mental illness. He declined to provide a supporting letter and told no one but Michael.
    Unprofessional and lazy. Get off your backside and find out, be curious. Smoke now coming out of the double barrels of my nostrils. The psychiatrist did not know Michael well.

Michael, of course, went down a different path. He was a man on a mission to get a gun. The Coroner found Michael had clearly failed to disclose his mental illness on the Victorian Firearm Licence Form he completed. He denied having treatment in the past five years.
    I am still fuming. Should I perhaps write to the

psychiatrist and ask if he understands what 'a duty of care' means? The police were totally unaware of Michael's history when his gun licence was granted. What is the law?

The **Firearms Act 1996** requires that a 'fit and proper person test' be applied to acquire a firearms licence. A record of mental illness and current medical evidence and advice would mean the person could fail the test. Section 183 of the **Firearms Act 1996** indicates health professionals are not subject to any civil or criminal liability for providing certain information to the Chief Commissioner provided the evidence is given in good faith. The law has not changed since Michael's death.

What has changed, if anything?

In February 2016 Victoria Police issued an information guide entitled 'The Role of Health Professionals in the Firearms Licensing Process.'

I wondered, could these guidelines have prevented someone like Michael getting a gun?

The guidelines inform health professionals on how and when to VOLUNTARILY report a patient to Victoria Police whom they deem unsuitable to hold a licence.

It got worse.

Victoria Police have an expectation that health professionals would notify them.

Would Michael's psychiatrist have responded to voluntary reporting and expectations?

I showed the guidelines to a friend who is a psychiatrist; he was unaware of them. We became curious as to how health professionals would know they exist.

My psychiatrist friend and I went searching on the websites of the Department of Human Services and the Royal Australian and New Zealand College of Psychiatrists.

We could only find the guidelines on the Victoria Police website.

My plea is for mandatory reporting to prevent people like Michael getting a gun.

PART TWO

Connections

Searching

My research about the origins of the significance of 'silhouette' and my quest to find answers to other bewildering episodes took me back to my childhood.

I was ill as a child which made me feel different and vulnerable, but my family became very protective and supportive of me.

When I was ten years old, I was diagnosed epileptic. The first time I was sunburnt I had two seizures whilst watching blurred television. I am very fair with an almost albino complexion and was taught to be very careful in the sun. The day of the burned skin was not sunny but windy, so my sister and I were tricked by the power of the wind. It was 1960 and at this time epilepsy had a stigma attached to it. Although only ten I went off to libraries to research my condition. The thing I was pleased to discover was that there were some important and famous people who also suffered this condition, but who managed to thrive in spite of their illness. My search for answers continued, as to how I would cope with my illness.

Swallowing my medication was the hardest thing to deal with. My sister Kay used to meet me every lunchtime in the toilets at school to throw my pills down my throat. My friends thought it weird that I disappeared to meet my sister in the dunny but at the time they did not know why because I didn't tell them.

It was probably the stigma of being ill and different that trapped me into secrecy. I had just started at a new school – Methodist Ladies' College – and probably was seeking acceptance. I just wanted to fit in. I met my sister every day on my 'pill parade' for about six months. Then a challenge: I was invited to stay overnight at my friend's house. Mum talked to me about telling my friend and her parents as they needed to understand in case anything happened. How could I take my pills by myself? My secret was out.

I was anxious of being rejected at first, but it turned out OK because my friend was a good pill thrower. After that my friend came on library visits with me to read up more on convulsions and what to do if they happened.

I had no more seizures and my annual visits to the neurologist showed clear EEGs. It seemed I was well generally and the epilepsy diagnosis did not stop me playing sport and all other school activities.

The greatest quandary for me about the label epilepsy was the prospect of being excluded from careers like teaching or social work, which I was interested in following. Mum and Dad took me to our local GP to talk about these worries of mine. I wanted to find out if there would be hurdles concerning career choices. I was sixteen at the time and the doctor reviewed my medication. He discovered that I had remained on a child's dose of the medication which the doctor thought was unusual. Our GP said he would liaise with the neurologist.

It was finally agreed by the neurologist that not increasing the medication had been an oversight. There was discussion about a misdiagnosis and maybe it was the sunburn and blurred television that led to those two seizures.

I was relieved by the revelation. My parents were angry that I'd worn the label of epileptic and taken seven pills a day for six years. Dad talked of suing the neurologist.

The medication was stopped and nothing happened. No more seizures. The neurologist thought the history of my case – only two seizures, clear EEGs and the child's dose of medication – would not prevent me seeking jobs or a career path.

For six years of my adolescence I lived with what I thought was a brain defect. My response was to be a diligent student and to try to excel at sport.

I'd defined myself as different and accepted this because of my illness. My strong family connections were a great help. I began wondering about labels such as 'epilepsy' and 'mental illness' and their effect on people. In a way I thrived on being different. Maybe this was an omen of other unusual choices I was to make in my life.

Michael and I made an early decision not to have children when we teamed up. We both wanted career paths and to travel the world together. Our love for each other was enough. I was not maternal and having a baby was never a yearning I held. Changing nappies and enfolding young children has never appealed to me.

Michael loved children, but was happy about my total lack of interest in being a parent. We were child-free by choice. This decision was cemented when I became pregnant, after failed contraception, at the age of twenty-three. We chose a termination. Our choice for Michael to have a vasectomy after my pregnancy was clear for us. Someone said to me, one of the interesting counterpoints of this decision would be the prospect of aloneness, especially in older age. It didn't happen. In my case, being child-free was offset by having a 'good family' of close friends. It was like an alternative togetherness because I had the energy to nourish and love my close friends and share our lives. I also wondered if close friends were more reliable than middle-aged children because of the support they provide.

Michael did not appear to be sad about being child-free because we were deeply blended in the lives of our many nieces and nephews and my god-daughter when they were growing up. We shared happy times with them without having to change nappies or be parents. We took these children to live theatre in the park, to concerts and to dinners where they could try exotic foods. Michael's four nieces used to visit him at the Automotive Industry Authority, where he was the Research Director, and he would take them to lunch.

We were also close to our two special nieces who lived in Canada as their father, Michael's young brother, died when they were children. They were international students whom we met up with in Norway, Italy and Scotland, during visits to Canada and on their trips to Australia. Their mother, Coops, was my best friend. I met her in 1961 at school and our lives have been close ever since. We met the Wynne-Hughes brothers, Michael and John, in 1970 at Monash University and they wooed us with food and wines. These friendships became significant as we married the brothers and became sisters-in-law. Close bonds continued even though they moved to Canada in 1977. We met up somewhere overseas every year. Coops is still an important buddy and although we do not see each other often, the conversation continues where we left off. She was nicknamed 'legs eleven' because she had skinny legs and she became a leg sister to me, sleeping in the same bed together all tangled up. The importance of close friendships was usually the key to my coping with stress or pain.

Michael did not have close friends apart from his brother John, who died when he was forty.

John and Coops invited us to Canada to spend Christmas with them because John was dying. It was painful to see him. He was a skeleton because the cancer had eaten away his body. John was angry about dying. Michael was overwhelmed by grief. John died six weeks later. Michael's pain stared loudly on his face. With hindsight this tragic event was probably another stepping stone on Michael's path to despair.

I became very interested in researching the grief literature because of the deaths of my sister Kay and brother-in-law John. I was studying psychology and social work at this time. An important text I was discovering and studying was the work of Dr Elisabeth Kübler-Ross and her book *On Death and Dying*. She is a well-known thanatologist and psychiatrist and this text was a treasure trove of new ideas about loss, grief and death and helping bereaved people.

Michael and I both read this text and it helped us to understand the stages in the grief process. An awareness of normal emotional responses to loss assisted us to realise grief is an individual journey.

At this time I had a placement at Pentridge Prison, working as a social work student. The text of Kübler-Ross was very relevant in the prison context too. Prisoners suffer extreme loss being separated from loved ones. Coping with loss was key to them surviving the prison experience.

After Michael died I reread *On Death and Dying* because

I wanted to see if it would help my bereavement. Books and research are such a comfort.

I'd been on a roller-coaster ride of lows and highs for me since Michael's death. It was essential for me to understand grief as a process, not just an event, even though my grief had been triggered by an event. Denial, anger, bargaining, depression and acceptance have all bruised me. But the stages of my emotional response did not happen in a linear way. What I didn't embrace was the concept of closure. People kept asking me if I had found closure.

I am not sure what 'closure' means. Maybe it is an acceptance of Michael's decision to kill himself. It seems superficial somehow because there can never be closure. I was still connected to Michael by memories of our life together. Someone suggested to me another way to think about grief and sorrow is that they are what you inevitably bear for the loss of what you loved. Maybe sorrow is an expression of lost love and a way to remember. Closure was a myth as a step in my grief process. I want to be connected through memories. I am wearing Michael's watch now.

Each individual has to work it out for themselves. Emotions will be influenced by things like religious beliefs, values and experiences. Surrounding yourself with warm caring people can help.

I was falling in love with Luctus. He listened to me without judgement. Soothing Luctus and his kindly smile made me feel safe.

Mr friend Amanda O'Connell was soothing for me. She lost her husband at the age of forty. Her grief was profound and the prospect of bringing up four children alone was daunting for her. I tried to listen to her pain. We were both social workers and knew about the theory of the grief literature.

Just after Michael died Amanda gave me a photo of Michael and me taken at Apollo Bay in 1976 when we were happy together. I felt I was being given a precious gift. Laughter was in our eyes as we hugged each other in our denim clothes. A '70s' photo.

She cherished fond memories of her beloved husband, Rob, at O'Connell family celebrations: 21st birthdays and weddings of their children. Her lost love gave her strength and courage. Amanda shared her vulnerability along her tough path. Her four children still talk about Rob because they are connected to memories of him.

After Michael died she also gave me keys to her house and always welcomed my presence in whatever emotional state I was in. Amanda remarried – Peter. They both knew Michael well and understood his pain and my sadness. Our shared histories and similar professional interests enabled conversations about loss and sorrow to flow. I was at home with them. After the theatre or book club I stayed at their house in South Yarra. Our conversations about vulnerability needed no explanations, and never will.

Lessons Learned from Dad

I wanted to talk to my dad after Michael died as he had always helped me through tragic and difficult times. Did my background help prepare me for the sudden death of my husband? I wondered if the eulogy given at my father's funeral answered this question. I called it 'Lessons Learned from Dad'. I need to include the sentiments I shared at Dad's funeral because it is part of my silhouette and it was written from my heart.

> *I must have been about ten when I began tagging along with Dad on home visits to Legacy widows and children who had no dads.*
>
> *It was during the film nights and barbeques at Stanhope and Blamey House (which were Legacy residences), where I watched him interacting with girls and young women, that my great fortune was brought home to me. I had a special father who joked with and helped these girls who had no fathers because their fathers had died. I observed him in action and what was apparent was the knack he had of making people feel worthwhile and special as they coped with their trials. I felt privileged to have Dad*

as my father. He was a man of integrity with a kind and generous nature.

Dad's legacy is the wise lessons I have learned from him and the values he instilled in me as a child.

The first lesson was the importance and value of community service. This was epitomised by his Legacy work and contributions he made in the community at Camberwell. He had a great influence on me, particularly in my career choices as a teacher, social worker and correctional administrator. I always chose to work with outsiders and marginalised people. What a great role model he was.

Growing up in Donna Buang Street, Camberwell, as part of a close-knit nuclear family with four kids was fun. We had happy childhoods. Dad and Mum were supportive and loving and really provided great foundations for us four kids to develop and grow. Our home was welcoming and was a great haven for our many friends. It was a place where people talked, listened and argued. It was a safe environment to test and share ideas and views.

Dad was my Rock of Gibraltar and it was not until adversity struck our family that this became apparent. My sister died suddenly of an aneurysm when she was eighteen and I still remember that night. I was at a party when the phone call came and I scurried home to be told Kay had died. I was met by Dad on the front veranda and we stood together hugging and crying. Amidst my tears I piped up that I would make up for the two of us. He said, 'No you will not. I just want you to be your beautiful self.'

Dad taught us the importance and value of sustaining long-term friendships. I still have fond memories of going to 'Dads and Daughters' lunches at the MCG with Dad, his army friends and their daughters over many years.

Another lesson came from watching him in action organising events and trips. He had exceptional organisational skills which became apparent in the compilation of OBSERVATION POST which is the history of the 2/11th Australian Field Regiment to which he belonged. A small committee accepted responsibility for the book which took some three years to complete. In the foreword, Lieutenant Colonel Entink wrote that the major credit must be given to Bill Lewis. 'Bill achieved the comparatively rare distinction of a Field Officer status in the Middle East. Perhaps it has been those qualities that distinguished his war service that served him so well in this task. His initiative, persistence and sheer hard work have paid handsome dividends in this volume.'

OBSERVATION POST was important to Dad. It was his legacy to us, his children and grandchildren. He wanted us to know about it. My copy is inscribed: 'Hope this meets with your approval. Love Dad.'

Dad taught us the importance of choosing well – be

it a footy team such as his beloved Demons or life partners. I do not know if he chose the best footy team but he remained loyal to his team. I do know he chose loving and caring partners.

Dad remarried in 1982 and with his wife they were able to share the next 25 years together after the deaths of their spouses. I am not sure what Rona made of the Lewis Clan in the beginning as we were a very argumentative family. Those family dinners were a riot. We all had plenty to say about war, politics and religion and being rowdy and not always listening was part of it. She coped.

The last four years or so have been somewhat harrowing as Dad's health deteriorated. The lung operation and hip replacement, however, created other opportunities. It enabled my older brother, Geoff, and me to travel to Queensland to assist Dad with his convalescence. His courage and determination were at the fore whilst he embarked on his recovery. We will never forget his determination to gain his strength again. It was during those weeks that I realised how many people's lives he had touched and the cards, the flowers and the kind wishes enabled my brother and me to realise how special he had been to so many people.

The last few months had been difficult for Dad. I was fortunate to be with him when he died peacefully on Saturday. Dad would say he had a good innings and *we will treasure our memories of him. I hope you can too.*

'Thanks for all the lessons, Dad, and I hope you think we are good students.' (April 2006)

Lily and I are nestled in my red tree.

'The Champagne Box' a piece of decoupage I created.

In my library in front of the portrait of my father.

My recently decorated living room.

Michael's 50th birthday plate which I designed celebrating the things he loved.

Bereavement Bonding

My father and I had parallel bereavement experiences, but we were at different life stages when these three sad events occurred in our family. How did we both cope?

Dad was forty-five years old when my sister Kay died. I have shared that she was eighteen years old. It was a sudden death. Losing a child is not in the expected order of things and my parents were heartbroken and bereft. I was seventeen years of age when I lost my shared childhood with my dear sister. We had slept in the same bedroom all our lives and she was no longer there to share our secrets.

We were a close family who shared dinner together at the dining table every night. We sat in the same chairs all our lives with me between Dad and Kay. This was our family time to share our stories and bond. No eating in front of the television at our place.

Eating green vegetables was always Mum's thing, which was not helped by Dad's refusal to enjoy any vegetables. The drama occurred each Saturday lunch when Mum insisted on a roast and green vegetables and we kids were not allowed to leave the table or go to Saturday afternoon pictures until the greens were eaten. I learned from a young age how to beat the system. I would put the vegetables in my mouth and spit them into my red aluminium mug before putting them down the sink. My siblings did not catch on, but Dad did and said nothing. He colluded with me as he thought the drama unnecessary after a hard week's work. Off to the flicks I went. Mum didn't cotton on to my mischief because she was consumed by fury at our food refusal. Too busy banging pots and pans. After a plea from Dad, the Saturday green practice stopped.

Dad and I had a special bond. I remember when I was a child he would throw me in the air with joy. Our favourite game was me standing on his feet facing him while he held my hands and we would go meandering around the house. I squealed with delight and never tired of this game. A favourite childhood song we all sang together was 'Build Your House on the Rock', which comes from the Holy Bible, Matthew 7:24–27. Let me share this with you because it could be a metaphor for our firm foundations. We all delighted in singing this and doing actions to illustrate the folly of building on the sand. The sentiment of the song was to build on the rock and not upon the sand because when the rain falls and the floods come the house built on the rock will remain sturdy.

As children and in our teenage years we all worked in our newsagency business but I got bored serving customers and before long started doing the books and accounts. Dad soon let me order cards because I was interested in colour and design and convinced him I had design flair. Ordering books was next because I was an avid reader.

Another special connection I had with my dad was our hair. I would comb his hair every night and he would brush mine before bedtime stories, when he picked a book or made up our stories before sleep.

We had happy childhoods and teenage years in a warm and loving environment that was interrupted by Kay's sudden death. As a family we used to sing together and another of our favourite songs was 'Six Green Bottles Hanging on the Wall', as there were six of us. It was really a counting song for kids and it went like this…

> Six green bottles, hanging on the wall
> Six green bottles, hanging on the wall
> And if one green bottle should accidentally fall,
> There'll be five green bottles hanging on the wall.

In 1968 there were no longer six of us at home as my elder brother had married and Kay had died so we were now only four green bottles.

The saddest bereavement experience we shared was dealing with Mum's suffering. After Kay died, my young brother Rob and I would come home to find her still at the breakfast table. She had not moved all day. This went on for a month until I suggested that this was unfair on the rest of us. We were all struggling variously with our grief, but Mum clearly needed help with her pain and broken heart. She did not seek this. Her sadness and grief remained.

In 1972 Mum was diagnosed with cancer and Dad stopped working to care for her at home. I visited every day on my way to university and he had all kinds of questions about pads, pants and other devices as she was incontinent. That did not stop Dad sleeping in their bed until she died. I marvelled at the way he lovingly cared for her.

Dad was fifty-five years of age when Mum died, and I was twenty-three. Their shared life had vanished at the prime of their lives. Dad had worked long hours in his own newsagency business which allowed us four children to be educated at private schools. The school fees had just come to an end and my parents had been planning all kinds of travel adventures, but this was not to be.

My creative, quirky mother had gone before I really shared close time with her. She was an artist who loved painting and pottery and she was a keen gardener. Mum had a huge collection of bonsai which she tended lovingly. At the time, I was not interested in gardens and missed the opportunity to learn from her and share her passions.

Dad continued his work at Legacy and his army friendships were his salvation. Dad was not on his own for long before he met and married a Legacy widow. They were happy together for the next twenty-five years and spent most of their time travelling and enjoying each other. But there was more grief on the way for my father.

Dad was seventy-seven years old and I was forty-five when my younger brother Rob died. He was the second child my father had to bury. I was very close to my brother, not only because of our shared childhoods, but also we had similar professional interests and qualifications. Rob was diagnosed with leukaemia and died at home a year later when he was forty.

My father was really struggling with the way Rob dealt with his illness and treatment. Rob was a psychotherapist and he had three young children whom he wanted to be intimately involved in his dying experience. He had two sons aged seven and nine from one marriage and he had a third child aged three. Rob married this child's mother during his treatment in hospital.

Rob chose to die at home and we had a roster of care to enable this to happen. Even up to the night he died his sons were crawling around in bed with him. Dad disapproved of this approach as he thought the children were too young to be exposed to this trauma. But it was Rob's way and I finally convinced Dad to let it go as Rob's wishes were paramount.

With hindsight, Dad's age was probably a factor here as his generation seemed to have a different view of the inclusion of young children in the dying process.

I was closely involved in Rob's dying plan. He appointed me executrix of his Will and Estate as he regarded me as more steadfast than his former or current wife. A few days before his death, the seven people Rob had chosen to speak at his funeral met with me and the minister. I explained how Rob wanted proceedings to unfold. We worked out an approach if any of us was overwhelmed on the day.

Rob was buried in an open casket in his favourite gardening clothes with his treasured working tools on display in the pockets. The night before the celebration I went to the funeral parlour to check how he looked. I took off the makeup, trimmed his beard and ripped out the white frilly bits of ribbons in the casket. My brother would have approved. This was our third family funeral. Rob's dying plan worked emotionally for all of us. His three young sons spoke and the three-year-old climbed into the casket which showed he did not have fears. Many other children placed coins, chess pieces, flowers, gardening tools and other items that connected them to Rob in the casket. He loved children and had built many cubby houses for them.

We all managed to speak without being overwhelmed, probably because of our support plan. When his young son called out 'Go Hawks' and placed Rob's Hawthorn footy scarf in the casket, everyone clapped. It seemed so natural. As the coffin was taken away, I did not feel the pain and angst that were my previous experience at our family funerals.

I remember thinking of an awful moment at Mum's

funeral when the minister insisted on telling us that her wish had been that we children return to church. It was audacious but he probably figured he would never see us again and he did not. Even Dad was coming around. A month before Rob died Dad accepted that Rob's approach of inclusion and sharing the dying experience was moving and therapeutic to us all.

    I was fortunate that my wonderful father lived until he was eighty-eight years of age and during the last year of his life I visited him every Thursday and I gave him foot and hand massages. His eyes would light up when I arrived and he would have the massage oils ready for his treat. We always had a tactile closeness through our hair brushing and in his old age this continued with the massages he loved. I also used to read to him. He would have the current book out and it was like the bedtime stories he read to me as a child.

Travel Traumas and Triumphs

I wanted to remember the times when Michael's face glowed with excitement.

Michael loved telling old stories about life-threatening situations we found ourselves in when we went on travel adventures together. Michael would get a twinkle in his eye rekindling memories of happier and 'hairy times' that we had survived. The stories got embellished over time as his illness progressed. He told them with gusto. Michael smiled with glee. Maybe he wanted to remember the smart-arse Michael, the risk-taker, when his problem-solving skills had shone.

We both wanted to see and experience the world. Exploring exotic foods, learning about different political systems, different cultures quenched our thirst for knowledge. It was our joint curiosity that bonded us together and led to some 'hairy times'.

Thinking back now, it was probably foolish going to Laos in 1974 during the Vietnam War. Michael had been 'called up' to fight. But winning his case as a conscientious objector was his way of fighting.

Michael had a colleague from Monash University who worked at the Australian Embassy in Vientiane. We went to visit him and stayed at the Continental Hotel because this was where the foreign journalists reporting on the war gathered. Listening to their stories opened our eyes.

We had watched the violence every night on television in Australia in the '60s and '70s. But hearing about the civilian massacre at My Lai from journalists who were there was chilling. There were bloodcurdling stories about the napalm bombings in the jungles which not only maimed people but also had devastating effects on the environment. We were beginning to wonder about the wisdom of being in Laos.

At a Christmas Eve party in the embassy we got advice from the Australian ambassador about where to travel safely. He said travelling in a boat down the Mekong River the next day, on Christmas Day, should be safe. There was to be a 'kinda truce' because apparently the Pathet-Lao-Viet Cong troops and the allies were to 'down tools' so they could all go home for Christmas dinner. Take a picnic, the ambassador suggested.

Before we got on the boat on the Mekong River, we did organise a picnic – baguettes and other goodies because Laos had once been a French colony. A bag of grass made into a chocolate cake was dessert. This was legal at the time in Laos. I volunteered in our group of friends to be the scout on that 'trip' down the river. We were sitting on the boat deck in our bathers. Michael's bare hairy chest was soaking up the sun and his long hair and beard were blowing in the wind. As we travelled down the river we saw many 'eyes' poking through the reeds from the river banks. The locals were peering at us and probably thought we were just crazy Westerners on a joy ride.

We felt safe until the crossfire started. We scurried into the safety of the cabin on the boat. Apparently not everyone had gone home for Christmas dinner. The boat somehow dodged the bullets. We were scared and very pleased when the boat was moored. Back at the Continental Hotel that night I had to sit on Michael. He had hallucinations of spiders. From the bidet in the hotel room I watched over him vomiting and writhing. What was 'that stuff' in the cake? I wondered. We needed to be more careful.

He was very unwell, but we had booked a plane trip the next day from Vientiane to Luang Prabang, so we decided to travel on. It was an unpressurised meat cargo plane, so our ears popped and hurt. On our arrival I took Michael to see a 'doctor' at a so-called medical clinic. There were queues of war wounded and we were clearly in the way.

Michael did receive an injection to lessen his pain. There was nowhere to stay at Luang Prabang. The idea that we should have carefully planned this war zone adventure kept echoing. We decided to catch a bus to Chiang Mai in Thailand. The trip was terrible as I watched Michael sweating and writhing in pain. I thought his days were numbered; so did he. On the bus I found out there was an American hospital in Chiang Mai. The bus driver took us there. We were greeted by a nurse who spoke English, which was such a relief. Michael was admitted into the hospital and the tests began because we had money.

We felt powerless until the doctor arrived. An unbelievable coincidence unravelled. Michael had been at the same secondary school with the doctor in Geelong. Even in Michael's state they shared war stories. He was ever curious to find out more. Safety at last! Michael was in hospital for two weeks with double pneumonia and perforated eardrums. We learned a lot from the doctor about the healthcare system and how the Vietnam War impacted on neighbouring countries. He had worked there for a year and the hospital was well equipped. His frustration, and the main difficulty, was that the locals could not afford the tests and treatment. We had money so Michael was well cared for and finally recovered. We could now fly home as his ears had healed.

What did we learn from this experience?

Travelling in a war zone showed how naive, fearless and reckless we were. Seeing the ravages of war, poverty and hunger in Third World countries was an eye-opening experience. It was hard to believe how people survived such mayhem.

We had each other. We were connected – no, not just connected, but united. We were beautifully blended.

The experience in Laos did not daunt us but gave us a taste for travel.

At the end of 1976 we had borrowed $30,000 to renovate our kitchen in our house in St Kilda. I had the better idea of travelling before I was to begin my career in the public service. President Allende had been shot in Chile and people were disappearing mysteriously in Argentina, but we thought as a team we would be OK. Off we went on our adventure to explore Latin America.

The bribery was the hardest thing for us to understand. We spent a lot of time reading our books in police stations. Wherever we went, the visas were wrong. They wanted a red stamp in our passports, not a black one. We had obtained all the visas in Australia. But the police thought we were white therefore wealthy, and they wanted us to pay for another stamp. We decided on no bribes. So we would sit reading in police stations until they realised we were not going to pay up. The police ultimately let us go.

This was until our experience at Copacabana near the border of Bolivia and Peru. We had hired bicycles and stupidly left them on the beach to walk up the pier to admire the vista. The bicycles were stolen. We reported the theft to the bicycle owner and he took us to the police station. With our broken Spanish, we ended up in custody, being accused of selling the bicycles. In the jail with open cells the indigenous Quechuan men were looking at me as though I came from another planet. I could not sleep there.

We sat in this custody arrangement for a few hours hatching a plan. We had to let someone know about our plight. Let the parents know where we were. We negotiated with the police, but we had to give up our passports. An armed escort took us to our hotel where we found there were no telephones, so ringing the parents or the embassy was not an option.

A Swedish couple saved us. We had met them earlier in our travels and they agreed to stick around until we were sorted and safe.

We gave them our money and took US$20 with us to begin the negotiation with the Police Chief. We knew it was always going to be about money. It was fortunate that his daughter, who spoke English, was there. She was educated at Oxford and came to our assistance.

We were scared but we were relieved the Police Chief's daughter cleared up the difference between stolen and sold. Miraculously, they had found the bicycles and now we had to pay for police time. We told them US$20 only, as we could not get money until we got to Peru. 'Perfect price,' he said. We left and after we crossed the border into Peru, Michael and I looked at each other and breathed a sigh of relief.

Good grief! We were thinking about how powerless we felt. Educated, white smart-arses, but in a foreign country in turbulent times – how vulnerable we were. Michael and I totally relied on each other. Our adversity bonded us. I started thinking about powerlessness and what it might feel like for the prisoners I was soon to encounter in my new home-town job. It was a humbling experience.

But this was not the end of our Latin American adventures. Trying to return to Australia from Chile was not what we expected.

It was January 1977. Why do I remember this detail? It is because I was to begin my new career in Corrections on 1 February 1977. After two magical months in Latin America we were heading home. At Santiago Airport, with the departure tax paid, we were left with $50. We had boarding passes for the plane trip to Easter Island, the first leg of our journey home.

Hanging around international airports is always a time for observation for me. I often wonder why and where people have been and imagine their stories. I love staring at people and making up their lives. Their appearance, their nationality and what they are reading often gives some clues.

Sometimes, I cannot help myself. My curious nature leads me to engage them in conversation to see if my observations have any merit. This was the case on our exit day from Chile. About half an hour before boarding time, couples were being called up to find they were 'bumped' from the flight. I was to learn there was a conference on Easter Island of Pinochet's army generals. No doubt, a party with the Americans to celebrate the assassination of the democratically elected President Allende. We assumed the generals, in all their regalia, were taking the seats of the travellers.

Fortunately, we were the last ones called because our surname is Wynne-Hughes and it seemed the 'bumping' was happening in alphabetical order. Time to hatch a plan. We had little money left and I needed to be on the plane to start my new job. Our problem-solving skills went into gear.

We decided not to go to the desk when they called our name. Our plan was to run onto the tarmac at the last boarding call and, still armed with our boarding passes, we would get on the plane at the very last minute. We did this. The hostess showing us to our seats said there must be a mix-up. The plane doors were closing which was all we cared about. We were on it and just hoped we would be allowed to remain. The generals were in our seats and we played dumb, which as a natural blonde I can do if the situation demands it.

I suggested sitting on the general's knee for the take-off and we could then share the crew seats because they would be busy and often out of their seats. The general did not mind because I was an attractive young blonde then. To our delight, the plane took off and we did take over the crew seats. But alas, that was not the end of this ordeal. In the confusion of the two extras on board, the hostess had not battened down the food trolleys properly and they went flying down the aisles. The crew apologised profusely as food splattered around. They decided the best way to placate the passengers was to provide free grog. It was like a party really, surrounded by generals in dress uniforms. By the time we arrived at Easter Island, most of the passengers were sloshed and there was much clapping and cheering on board. The hostess then explained we could resume our real seats as the generals departed.

What a weird place for a conference, as the island looked pretty barren except for those gigantic big boulders which were the feature of the landscape. Michael and I settled into our seats from Easter Island to Melbourne, the final leg on the trip, with a smile on our faces. We congratulated each other on our enterprising exit from Chile. Resourceful, quick wits who beat their corrupt system. It was a pity the Chileans had to suffer those harsh years with dictator Pinochet at the helm, with the violence and mayhem he created. Our $30,000 adventure in Latin America, instead of renovating the kitchen, had been a lesson in life and the ways of the world.

When we touched down in Melbourne, we both cried with relief in the knowledge we were safe in our stable country. We were both young and naive in some ways, but we were bonded in adversity and believed we would always be together. We were a formidable travelling team. We had experienced corruption, bullying and scary times in foreign lands, but learned lessons about powerlessness and humility.

There is one more tale Michael liked telling. We were in the Ardèche Valley in France in 1994. On a bright sunny day we watched people kayaking through the river valley and we thought the next day we would give it a go. We had no prior experience and the Frenchman who hired out the kayak to us spoke to us in French about 'très difficile' bends in the valley. We were not deterred and set off with our passports, keys and picnic in a plastic barrel. No helmets or safety equipment. It took about fifteen minutes before we met the first set of rapids which catapulted us out of the kayak, the oars were flung far and wide, and we watched our barrel disappear. This ordeal was to last for eight hours. We were in the water, battered and bruised by the rocks, and the only way to keep warm was to piss ourselves which we were doing anyway because we were both terrified. There was no passport and no keys – they were in the barrel. We were exhausted but found our barrel near the wharf. It was more than we deserved. The bus took us to our hotel.

We ordered the best burgundy available which we drank before climbing into bed for two days to let our wounds heal. This had been a very dangerous, reckless adventure. But we lived in togetherness to tell the tale.

The Bluestone Decades

Pentridge Prison on Sydney Road in Coburg is a feature on Melbourne's landscape. It was known as Bluestone College because it was built of bluestone slabs. It operated as Victoria's maximum security prison from 1851 until it closed in 1997.

The anti-capital punishment protests in the '60s first sparked my interest in prisons. The stony face of Pentridge Prison, with that giant clock tower, stared aggressively at me from our television screen during the demonstrations.

It was the hanging of Ronald Ryan, the last prisoner to be legally executed in Australia, that drove the protests. Ryan was found guilty of killing a prison officer, George Hodson, during an escape from Pentridge in 1965.

The Supreme Court Justice, John Starke, who sentenced Ryan to death, was an army friend of my dad. I had met him in 1967 and learned of his angst about the mandatory penalty he had to impose. The case was controversial and led to many heated debates around our dining room table at home and in the community. The protests did lead to the end of capital punishment.

My curiosity about Pentridge Prison was fuelled by these events and stayed with me. Pentridge Prison has a brutal history which I discovered reading the findings of The Jenkinson Inquiry in 1972–3. The conditions at the infamous high security 'H' Division at Pentridge were condemned. The government was forced to act and the impetus for change was beginning.

In early 1975 I invited the Superintendent of Pentridge Prison to Monash University. Social work students like me were encouraged to branch out and develop networks with community services and invite guest speakers of interest. This seemed like an opportunity to harness my curiosity and to find out the 'real' story. It led to my entry into the prison system.

I arrived at the main entrance to Pentridge Prison in 1975. I was to meet up with the Superintendent of Pentridge to begin my four month social work placement. It was a bit scary going through the gates. Keys jangled. Doors slammed. There were cold stares from the prison officers escorting me to see their boss. Solemn faces everywhere. A male, blokey domain, my intuition told me. Females unwelcome.

For four months I was based in the Classification Centre in the Southern Prison at Pentridge. This was the hub of the system because all prisoners received into custody came there for assessment and classification. The prisons in Victoria were classified as maximum, medium or minimum security. Once prisoners were sentenced, they would be given a security rating that determined which prisons across the state they could be sent to. Ordinarily, prisoners would start their sentence in maximum security, and work their way to minimum security, which meant better access to visits and pre-release programs.

My key task as a social work student was to design a standardised social history proforma that included the information required to assess prisoners and make placement decisions. And to my amazement, I discovered that though the prison officers wrote the reports, it was the classification 'billets' who prepared the files and typed up the reports – in other words, prisoners – and they had access to confidential information on fellow prisoners!

There is a hierarchy of offences amongst 'crims'. Sexual crimes that related to children are the bottom of the barrel. These prisoners are assessed for protection status to stop fellow 'crims' meting out their own vengeance on them. Protection prisoners need to be kept safe and the less people knew of the gory details of their crimes, the better. But a mischievous 'classo billet' (see page 125 for an explanation) could let the prisoner grapevine know this kind of information. No wonder professional psychiatrists, psychologists and social workers would only provide scant information on prisoners because the 'wrong' eyes could look at the information these professionals provided.

This task of designing the social history proforma introduced me to prison 'lingo' and etiquette. The blue doors were opening. It was a whole new language for me to learn.

Billets, van therapy, shanghais, classo, iron barred, bronzing up, rock spiders, slammer, Governor's Pleasure, lockdowns, musters, buddy cells and pre-let out traps were all new words to me, and I was keen to understand the darker shades of their meaning.

I wondered why prisoners had access to confidential information. In a word, money.

In 1975, Prisons Division was part of the Social Welfare Department which had to compete with children and adolescent services for resources. I soon discovered prisons were the lowest priority. Attempts to obtain resources to replace prisoner billets with civilian staff had been unsuccessful.

I was supervised on my placement by the Associate Professor of Social Work from Monash University as there were no social workers at Pentridge. I reported to the Superintendent of Pentridge who was a sociologist. My supervisors and I decided we desperately needed to take action to put pressure on the Social Welfare Department to provide civilian clerical resources. I wrote to the Minister for Corrections.

The original proposal I prepared was co-signed with the Associate Professor from Monash. We received a response saying it was on the list but there were more pressing priorities in the department. Over the next eighteen months, I kept up the lobbying but the Minister's responses were snail-like.

In February 1977 I became a public servant in the Social Welfare Department and I had been there only three weeks when I got hauled in to see the Director-General. My 'crime' was writing to the Minister. I was asked to withdraw my letter. I chose to comply rather than be sacked and prepared the same document for the signature of the Associate Professor who could lobby the Minister. Two years after we began this project, the prisoner billets were withdrawn and were replaced by civilian staff.

Prisoners could no longer use the grapevine to mischievously pass on information. It allowed us to improve the silhouettes of prisoners and incorporate 'mug shots of crims' into our files.

Well done. What a long slow process to get change. But successful.

Why do I want to talk to Luctus now about the work

that consumed me for twenty-one years? Maybe a listening ear would help me understand and differentiate between my professional and personal selves in dealing with loss and grief. Few people can work and stay in government jobs in Corrections without probing their motives. Did this structured, ordered, but often challenging environment suit me because I felt rewarded and acknowledged?

What were my motives to tackle this kind of work?

I began wondering what I would list if giving a PowerPoint presentation to school students.

- Was it 'dealing with lost souls' whose grief was unknowable?
- Was it trying to provide hope to prisoners and their families with bleak futures?
- Was it trying to understand the link between lack of self-worth and self-harming behaviours?
- Was it to resolve the quandary of whether unresolved loss and grief caused prisoners to choose such self-destructive paths?

You have a curious nature and a thirst for knowledge so all your questions and quandaries make sense.

There were very few females positioned around Pentridge in the 1970s. Clothing etiquette for females required us to be covered up because we were dealing with male prisoners and staff. People tell me I am remembered for my long blonde hair and colourful rainbow stockings. Pentridge was such a bleak, gloomy place and my stockings brought smiles to the faces of officers and prisoners.

This was in contrast to how I felt. When I went into the divisions to see prisoners or staff, I could smell the sweat and feel the pain that clung to the walls. It was not a place of hope.

My decades in custody can really be divided into four quarters, like the seasons. Each season had different professional and personal challenges. *The first quarter (1977–1982) was the 'summer' season of discovery* because I was learning the knots and ropes. I was one of the first female social workers in Prisons Division. Surviving in a male dominated workplace was a challenge, as any lone woman pioneer will know.

Initially the Governors and uniformed staff did not welcome social workers because they thought we were spies who would go back to head office and inform on them. They underestimated us. We wanted social justice, not just for prisoners, but for the staff too, because they were all together in dilapidated, under-resourced facilities. We were trying to break new ground, transforming closed institutions into places where accountability and fairness could become the norm. But I did not fool myself that I was a Nightingale, Pankhurst or prison reformer Elizabeth Fry.

My baptism of fire came working at Fairlea Women's Prison. The Governor was required to live there; she was like a prisoner herself. The Governor was resistant to change and hostile because she felt threatened by my challenging mind.

Our meetings were held in the multipurpose day room in the prison. It contained equipment for art classes and a piano for music lessons. My boss, Grant, was a concert pianist and he used to come to the prison before important meetings and play classical music to 'soften' the Governor. It worked.

I had first met Grant Johnson in 1975 at Pentridge Prison, just after he was appointed senior social worker – a memorable occasion. We were watching two notorious prisoners tending the rose garden outside the Governor's office. One was a heavy in the union movement and the other ran funeral parlours. They were leaning on their spades. We imagined the dialogue they were having and wondered if concrete boots were mentioned.

Grant and I were to become lifelong friends, and when he teamed up with his partner, Steven Wharton, we began our food and wine soirees. We had Sunday night tennis bouts at our home, BBQs and travels together when Steven would recite fables to us in French. Michael, who was well in those days, became Steven's mentor. They were great supports during Michael's illness and we are still closely connected.

I want to hear more about your work at the women's prison.

I was shocked to find we had a prisoner who lived in a cage because she had assaulted staff and the Governor thought this was the only solution. The secure cage was 4 metres x 4 metres in size. It kept the prisoner separate from staff and fellow prisoners. When I went to see her, we talked through the iron mesh because the Governor was concerned for my safety.

Prisoners are held in custody by a warrant which describes and names the prisoner and sets out the crime, conviction and sentence. We had a transsexual prisoner called Colin on her warrant. She was midway through her treatment changing her sex from male to female. She no longer had a penis. I was giving a presentation to staff concerning the management of transsexuals. My attempts to have Colin called Carol for her psychological wellbeing were in vain. In front of all the staff, the Governor told me, 'Women in here tell me they are Jesus Christ and I do not call them Jesus. We call prisoners by the names on their warrants.' A fair point in a way.

We also had two young pregnant prisoners. The Governor thought they got pregnant deliberately in an attempt to manipulate the sentencing judge to give them a lenient term. These two prisoners were convicted on serious drug charges and both received long sentences. I wondered if they would be able to keep their babies in prison. The babies' names would not be on the warrants. Though it can take time on social justice matters, I had faith that fairness would eventually bloom.

Two blossoms: finally the prisoner came out of the cage and Colin was allowed to be called Carol. We developed legislation to allow women to have their babies in custody and Victoria led the way in the world in this policy area. In the end, I became solid friends with the Governor who was finally allowed to live outside the prison. Just before she died, she invited me to Tasmania to play bridge and we laughed about my baptism of fire for which she apologised. I had already forgiven her as she taught me a great deal. Friendship, someone said, is a great facilitator of goodwill.

During the first quarter, I was also the social worker on the Work Release Program that was run out of a Church of England hostel for homeless men. The participants were long-term prisoners in the final months of their sentences. They had jobs in the community, and had to be in the hostel outside their work hours.

These long-term prisoners were often anxious when I was taking them from Pentridge Prison into their new home in the community. I spent two hours every week with each prisoner to listen to their feelings and concerns. Sometimes I met them at their workplace. Sometimes over a coffee. Helped them shop for presents and other simple everyday tasks. I saw the glazed look in a prisoner's eyes when we went on a tram ride. He was using decimal currency for the first time and wanted to examine the coins. One bank robber was uneasy because he was opening his first bank account and didn't know which queue to stand in. Such ordinary things were new to them. It was probably understandable because these prisoners had been disconnected from the community for decades.

Twice a week I had dinner at the hostel with the prisoners. It became our ritual. I was surprised to get a request from a prisoner to teach him to eat. This prisoner was called 'Bluey' because he had red hair. I was listening to him and he told me he watched me eating and loved my confidence. He commented, 'You seem to know what to do and are at ease at the table.'

Having experienced many meals with prisoners in custody where knives and forks were in the air I appreciated what was being requested. He was really asking me to show him table manners, the etiquette, how to be accepted when he was invited for dinner. Pondering this request, I thanked my mother who taught me what became known as my 'Miss Camberwell table etiquette'. We all laughed and the lessons started in earnest with all the eight prisoners who wanted to participate.

We started with setting the table and the first principle was outside in. Depending on the number of courses to be served, the table was set with soup spoons, main course knives and forks and dessert spoons in the order of the courses, starting with the soup spoon on the outer. They soon got this principle and it quickly went into action.

Next came waiting for all of us to be served before we began eating together. This was followed by finishing together before the plates were cleared. Watching these huge tattooed prisoners practising their new-found skills was a delight. 'How did I go? Did I do it properly?' They loved to be told they did well. It showed the importance of them being accepted with the ordinary tasks of life. We had a lot of fun and Miss Camberwell etiquette lessons became part of our program. Visits to the library to find books on table manners were a hit with the prisoners too.

Well done. These prisoners seemed to be 'at home' with you. I liked the way you helped connect them with their inner feelings. To name them and express them. Connections, belonging and acceptance are what they were seeking. You were giving them renewed hope so they could become a different self and engage in a new life.

One night a prisoner called Peter did not return to the hostel after work. I alerted the Governor of Security at Pentridge. I was about to go home at 9.30 pm and was sitting on the veranda waiting for my taxi. Another prisoner, John, alerted me to the fact that Peter was staggering up the long pathway to the hostel. The next thing that happened was the seven other prisoners surrounded me on the veranda. They wanted to protect me. John piped up, 'I will deck him, miss, so he can't hurt you.' 'No,' was my reply. I was feeling vulnerable and was wondering how I would deal with this situation. Peter had a history of violence and rape. He looked too drunk to do anything but he did have a knife. Fortunately Peter passed out before he reached the veranda. The security van appeared and Peter was taken back into custody.

I was grateful for my prisoner support team but was anxious that I had no back-up or security at the hostel. The program was run on a shoestring. I regret there was never any money to resource programs properly.

A highlight for me in my first quarter was being appointed as the first female Superintendent of an Attendance Centre. Four centres were set up as sentencing options for the courts for prisoners serving less than twelve months, so they stayed in their jobs and remained with their families. They attended the centre two evenings per week to participate in programs and undertook community work each Saturday. The community work projects were organised by my program supervisor. The jobs varied and he matched the offender to the client.

Once a month I would go and see some of the work. I remember meeting Miss Phillips at her place. When I arrived she was sitting on her front veranda with the offender, Peter, having high tea. The dainty bone china cups were on display. The teapot was piping hot and so were the biscuits she had made for him. I joined them. Peter had weeded the garden, done the lawns and odd jobs at her place for nearly a year. Miss Phillips asked me if Peter would be allowed to continue visiting her after his term expired in two weeks' time. They were both eager. Peter continued working at her place and enjoying high tea with this isolated, elderly woman. They had a caring connection until she died some two years later.

I had only one humiliating experience as Superintendent. It happened at the Preston Magistrates' Court while I was prosecuting a case on behalf of the Department for an offender who had breached his program conditions. We were not trained lawyers and the Department would only pay for lawyers to represent us in the County Court. It was my first 'breach' and of course the offender had a barrister who questioned my delegation to perform this role. We lost the case but the Department decided to pay for us to be trained and we soon got the right delegation to prosecute cases.

My experiences in Corrections did provide unintended learning opportunities. I started wondering if I should write a dictionary of prison lingo.

I started my list and here it is:

- A muster is a term used to describe a headcount of prisoners.
- A billet is a prisoner clerical assistant.
- Van therapy is when a troublesome prisoner is moved to another prison location to avoid trouble.
- Shanghais are prisoners returned from country prisons to Pentridge for reclassification (usually without proper authority).
- Classo is short for classification which is a placement decision.
- Slammer is a prison cell in 'H' Division.
- Rock spider is a term to describe a prisoner who is willing to be sexual prey.
- Iron barred is when a prisoner is assaulted with an iron bar.
- Buddy cell is a term used to describe a purpose-built cell designed to accommodate two prisoners for the purpose of providing each other with peer support.
- Lockdown is a term used to describe the situation

where prisoners are locked in their cells for a significant proportion (up to 23 hours) of a 24 hour day.

- Pre-let out trap is a term used to describe a small lockable trapdoor located within the cell door used by prison officers to conduct prisoner counts while prisoners are locked in their cells.
- Observation regime is a term used to describe the level/frequency of observation a prisoner is to receive for a given time period.
- At risk is a term for those prisoners with an increased probability of attempting suicide or self-harm.

The Department did encourage us to study criminology, so I went to Melbourne University part-time for four years. It was time for me to reflect on the role of Corrections in the criminal justice system. I was fascinated to study the United Nations International Covenant on Civil and Political Rights. This set me thinking about guiding principles to inform our work concerning prisoner rights.

I was also introduced to the language and practices concerning the detention of mentally ill prisoners and people detained at the Governor's Pleasure. Quaint language. Which governor and whose pleasure? I found these people were detained indefinitely by the Governor of Victoria. They were either unfit to plead or were found not guilty of the crimes (usually murders) they committed on the grounds of insanity at the time of the commission of the offences. In 1978, why were twenty-one of these people in prison? These people needed treatment in a psychiatric hospital rather than a prison. I wanted to find out where they were located.

Being appointed the Supervisor of Classification with

a delegation to transfer and place prisoners provided this opportunity. I chaired the Classification Committee which met each Monday in the Classification Centre Board Room. The table was a semicircle of dark panelled wood around which the committee members sat.

The prisoner being interviewed sat in the middle of the circle. The back wall consisted of a giant blackboard which listed all the prisons and identified where there were vacant beds. It was a daunting place. I used to interview prisoners here each Friday to help prepare them for the meeting they were to attend in the boardroom when they would be classified.

The toughest decisions concerned the high security prisoners located in 'H' Division and Jika Jika in the Pentridge complex. These units had their own Review & Assessment Committees because the prisoners could not be moved out of their locations for security reasons. I chaired these committees too. We interviewed the prisoners on a regular basis to see them and let them have a VOICE. My news about future placement options was often bleak.

There was a prisoner I'll call Andrew in 'H' Division. He was serving a sentence of natural life for the murders of two people. He was diagnosed as schizophrenic. Andrew was due to attend the Review & Assessment Committee that day. A psychologist had seen Andrew that morning. The prisoner had covered himself in his own excrement. This is known as 'bronzing up', usually as a form of protest or a plea for help. Andrew had then sprinkled talcum powder over the excrement. He had told the psychologist he was a 'lamington' and wanted to go to hospital. Andrew had a history of eating bucket handles and razor blades and other forms of self-abuse. From time to time he had been transferred to Mont Park Psychiatric Hospital for treatment. I wondered if he would meet the requirements of the Mental Health Act. Probably not, because he wasn't psychotic… he just felt like a lamington.

It was frustrating that our staff had to deal with the so-called mad or bad prisoners. We knew there was a better solution than my advocating on their behalf or sometimes begging for proper treatment for these struggling souls. I wondered how this policy area could become a frontier for reform.

In 1980 the Jika Jika high security unit was opened in the Pentridge Prison complex. It was like a separate prison within a prison. Its claim to fame was it had won an 'Excellence in Concrete Award'. The building was yellow in colour and on my first visit it felt like being in a submarine. It reminded me of the joy in the lyrics of the Beatles song 'Yellow Submarine'. In stark contrast, there was no joy in Jika Jika.

The design of Jika Jika was based on the idea of six separate units at the end of radiating spines. The units comprised electronic doors, closed-circuit TV and remote locking to keep staff costs to a minimum and security to a maximum. The furnishings were sparse and prisoners exercised in caged yards.

Limited fresh air, computerised door openings, double-glazing everywhere and paraphernalia to prevent prisoners and prison staff interacting – it felt like sensory deprivation to me and I wondered what the staff and prisoners would feel. At least in 'H' Division, even with its hateful history, staff and prisoners interacted, keys jangled, doors and gates slammed. They could communicate. I remember the Governor of 'H' Division telling me he cooked up onions and bacon outside the cells of prisoners on hunger strikes as a means to encourage them to eat. It was a pity this somewhat tempting torment could not happen in Jika Jika.

My task was to transfer the prisoners from 'H' Division to Jika Jika safely and securely. I went back to headquarters and spoke to the Director-General about my impressions of Jika Jika. Why had we built a concrete submarine? I wondered.

In no uncertain terms, I was told to keep my opinions to myself as $7 million had been spent in designing this new age facility which would cope with future terrorists and high security prisoners.

I soldiered on, transferring the prisoners from a hellhole of history to the new age concrete mass with its hi-tech devices and electronics. But I was able to engage the Criminology Department at Melbourne University to set up a research project to monitor the placement of prisoners. I knew the value of independent scrutiny, accountability and transparency in decision-making.

Did I just write that sentence? It sounds so formal but my workplace demanded bureaucratic language. The prison system had a culture of denying emotions and of keeping emotional distance. It was a dehumanising environment that did not sit well with my own emotional self. The plight of some of these prisoners was gut-wrenching. My professional self put on the cloak of authority. My personal self was put away, for now.

For the prisoners, the Jika Jika experience was about extreme loss. It was not only the deprivation of liberty for these prisoners but also the loss of air, human contact and spirit. Attempts were made by the welfare officer to provide this place with a soul and all sorts of organisations and people wanted to come and participate. The intrigue was enormous but we had a duty of care to ensure we acted in the best interests of the prisoners.

For example, one group wanting to help out was an ashram in Fitzroy that wanted to teach yoga. I decided the best way to check out their bona fides was for my husband and me to do cooking classes with them. They were assessed and we allowed them to teach yoga; they stayed and had a calming influence on the prisoners. In addition, mutual support programs, like Alcoholics' Anonymous, and Gamblers' Anonymous, were helpful as despairing people can be assisted when they appreciate they are not alone on their journeys.

Learning the ropes at work did lead to self-understanding. The culture of denying emotions was probably a coping mechanism to deal with heart-wrenching situations. Writing in bureaucratic formal language when describing painful events was a self-protection mechanism.

Emotional distance influenced my personal life too. When Michael and I had ups and downs in our marriage, our situation led me to wonder about the language between couples. How well do we listen to each other when we are busy? I squeezed fresh orange juice each morning and gave Michael breakfast in bed. But how did I react after an argument? I had to be aware of my emotional withdrawal when hurt.

The Creative Quarter (1983–1988) was my autumn. A new Labor government had been elected. The Office of Corrections was established with its own resources to manage the thirteen Victorian adult prisons and community corrections. Maybe the autumn leaves were turning because the Minister for Corrections had permission to set a new agenda.

The lasting legacy of this period was the formulation of a sound legislative base. It was a once-in-a-lifetime opportunity to write a whole new Act of Parliament to provide governance for Corrections in Victoria. What were the key policy issues that were likely to be contentious with uniformed staff and prisoners?

I wrote a list outlining some scenarios for the new Director-General because he came from Western Australia and each prison jurisdiction has a particular history that needs to be understood.

I wrote this list for consideration:

1. Firearms in prison.

    The last prison officer killed by prisoner Ronald Ryan in 1965 was indelible in the Corrections corporate memory. Should firearms be abolished in prisons?

2. Children in custody.

    How long should a baby or child be able to remain in custody?

    A recent case of a sachet of heroin in a baby's nappy after the prisoner had a contact visit brought home competing demands. What is in the best interests of the child versus security and safety issues in the prison?

3. Prisoner rights.

    The new government wanted these identified and enshrined in legislation for the first time. What should they be?

4. Hunger strikes.

Bobby Sands (1954–1981) was an Irish member of the Provisional Republican Army who died on a hunger strike whilst imprisoned at HM Prison Maze in Ireland. His death and those of nine hunger strikers was followed by a surge of IRA recruitment and activity.

Bobby Sands and his death led to copycat events in Victoria and elsewhere.

Do you let a prisoner die?

5. Hostage negotiations.

What is the role of the police if a prisoner takes a hostage in a prison?

6. AIDS.

The AIDS epidemic had started. Prisons were thought to be incubators for the disease because prisoners shared needles and had unprotected sex. Should HIV status prisoners be kept in a separate prison?

7. Gazettal of prison sites.

Should the adjoining land to prisons be gazetted as part of the prison site to allow flexibility to house prisoners in tents when there were no vacant beds? We often had no beds and this led to 'Operation Sardine' solutions.

8. Strip searching of prisoners.

What protocols should apply to protect the privacy of prisoners yet allow hidden drugs to be found?

9. Use of force.

In what circumstances should prison officers be authorised to use force?

The situations you played a role in at work seem to have a recurring theme of negotiating boundaries. Competing interests and dilemmas are all grey areas that need solutions.

The Director-General and I spent three years developing and consulting widely about policy issues. The **Corrections Act 1986** and the Corrections Regulations were finally passed by Parliament.

We were also given permission to plan, design and build four new prisons and close old, dilapidated facilities. What a great opportunity it was to be creative and clever in designing purpose-built facilities that could enable improved care and management of prisoners. We could put into practice policies to prevent suicides. Sightlines for supervision, reduction of hanging points in cells and building communities of care were all aspects of that improvement.

When the AIDS epidemic broke out in the early 1980s, people were terrified that prisons would be incubators of the disease. It seemed AIDS was transmitted by blood. Prisoners sharing needles when injecting drugs and unprotected sexual activity were both obvious areas of concern. Prison systems across the country went into panic mode. Do we need to separate prisoners with an HIV status? Do we need a separate prison for so-called contaminated prisoners? What are the risks for our staff? Who knew the answers? No one.

I joined a National Prisons Committee to try to work out a response and strategy to an unknown fear. The Grim Reaper advertisements appeared and we were all struggling for solutions. It was serious because no one had the answers. There was much discussion about introducing male condoms into prisons, as the 'cling wrap' the prisoners used during sex would not be effective in curtailing the spread of the disease. How best to implement controversial policy?

I was sent on a mission to one of our medium security country prisons for long-term prisoners that had a private visit facility where prisoners could have conjugal visits. Should we try to introduce condoms there as a starting point? The Governor was a burly, huge ex-shearer by trade who had his own way with words. I was sent to convince him this trial with condoms could be groundbreaking. I was to discover he had been wisely providing condoms in the private visit facility for the past ten years to prevent pregnancy. I always loved the resourcefulness of our Governors. I congratulated him on his initiative and he agreed to be our champion for introducing male condoms in prisons.

I had a dilemma when the first HIV positive prisoner came into prison. Where to safely place him? I consulted with the medical staff and he was placed in the hospital at Pentridge. That night the medical officer went home. His wife sent him back to Pentridge clad in a blanket. She had burnt his clothes to shield herself and the children from the germs. Such was the ignorance then and the fear of the unknown.

At this time in 1984, Victoria was hosting the Annual Conference of Ministers for Corrections to debate and share issues of concern. HIV was the topic and condoms and needle exchange were the main agenda items. I organised for a condom company to give a presentation on male/male condoms. We were in la-di-da surroundings at the Regent Hotel in Collins Street with chandeliers on the ceiling and plush red carpets. The display consisted of ceramic penises of different sizes and they showed us the length and strength of different male/male condoms. The funniest thing for me, as the only female present, was the total naivety of my male colleagues. None of them had ever used condoms and they watched the instructor showing the technique of application with great interest. It was the early '80s, but boys, I am told, never like a shag in a shower cap so their inexperience was probably understandable.

Just as well the Office of Corrections did have a sound legislative base because 1987 was a turbulent year. Our Emergency Procedures were tested by a hostage situation and a tragic fire.

<u>Hostage Scenario</u>, August 1987. A prisoner took six teachers and three prisoners hostage in the Education Centre at Bendigo prison, a medium security facility. I took out the Emergency Procedures Manual 'Dealing with Hostages in Prison'.

1. Set up the Emergency Control Room at headquarters.
2. Alert Chief Commissioner of Police.
3. Establish link with police negotiator and the hostage taker.
4. Alert the Executive members of the Office of Corrections.
5. Log the demands and dialogue between the police negotiator and the hostage taker as events unfolded.

The prisoner allegedly had a gun and an incendiary device around his neck. He was threatening to blow up the prison. He wanted to be called 'The Anti-Nuclear

Warrior'. His demands were for a nuclear free world and improvement in prison conditions.

There were going to be long nights and days in the Emergency Control Room. Better get some stretchers to sleep on. The Director-General was clear about the outcome to the police negotiator. Hostages and hostage taker out alive, if at all possible.

I knew a number of the teachers well. A gut-wrenching experience, wondering about their welfare and safety.

The dilemmas posed were what risks do you take with the lives of the hostages? Should the police shoot the hostage taker?

The siege lasted for 46 hours. The hostages were not physically hurt but the psychological and emotional toll was high. The hostage taker was returned to high security for the investigation. The teachers were traumatised.

Jika Jika Fire, 29 October 1987. A fire in Jika Jika resulted in the tragic deaths of five prisoners. They had barricaded themselves in and lit the fire. Staff and emergency service personnel were not able to free them.

The next day Jika Jika was closed as a prison and a chapter ended. But a lonely wintery chapter was beginning with dark clouds accumulating because a spate of inquiries began. It was time to be accountable. How could this have happened? I wondered how to deal with professional loss and grief that demanded my emotional distance. How was I to protect myself from the pain and angst of others?

Meanwhile, my domestic situation was in turmoil too. Michael and I had our separation in 1987. We had sold our property and gone on our ways. Our lives had been entwined for fifteen years. I struggled living alone. I felt like an octopus that had been sliced down the middle.

All those tentacles in our life had been untwined, but raw nerve ends remained exposed, like wounds that were red and puffy. I wondered if grief is love that has no other place to go. I wondered if pressing love and pain together might produce wisdom.

The structure and order in my life was still my consuming passion for work, even in volatile times. Although the inquiries were taxing, we had to keep moving instead of getting stuck.

The winter of my correctional career, I remember, was the Planning Quarter (1988-1992) where a few buds were appearing. The coffers of government looked bare. I soldiered on with my networks with permission to reform health and education services in prisons.

A spate of hangings in prisons caused alarm bells. I examined each case to find hanging points in cells were the common thread. One prisoner was hanging from the shower screen rod in his cell. Another from the door handle on a cupboard. Another from shoelaces tied to a bed. Hanging points in cells needed to be examined. Physical change in cell design and cell furniture might make a difference.

But how to deal with prisoners who were assessed because they were 'at risk' of suicide. Placing them in a padded observation cell near the prison officers' station was not really the answer. 'Suicide watches' by prison officers checking on prisoners every half an hour could become invasive and dehumanising.

What about assessment procedures – are the health and corrections staff working as a team? Are there barriers to communication? Who knew what information about the prisoners found hanging? How could these quandaries be tackled?

Exploring solutions to these big questions sent me back to 1975, my early exposure working with people who had made suicide attempts. As part of my social work course I spent a four month placement at The Alfred Hospital. My research project was in the Psycho-Social Assessment Clinic, working with a psychiatrist and social worker. I followed up patients who had made a suicide attempt, to offer assistance and support. The care philosophy of early intervention with despairing people might prevent suicides, if appropriate care, kindness and treatment could be offered.

I began wondering about what the tread to suicide might feel like for patients. Meanwhile, during 1988 Michael was suffering from depression and I was delving into the literature to find out how to help him. Michael attended appointments with psychiatrists to obtain his medication that stabilised his mental illness.

After these sessions he would report to me about the psychiatrists he had interviewed. He had found out their favourite wines, food preferences and restaurants they liked. He toyed with them to avoid acknowledging his own vulnerability.

Michael hated the fog the medication created in his big brain. He was intellectual and our friends thought he was the cleverest man they had ever met. He was brilliant and could put a fine case in any debate or argument, particularly those concerning economics and politics. He hated the side effects of that wretched medication. So did I. Meanwhile, I soldiered on at work.

I have sketched some of the complex prisoner health

issues. Mad or bad prisoners were in a 'limbo' between psychiatric hospitals and prison with scarce resources to provide care. I felt I was in a limbo between the psychiatrist's medication and support I was struggling to provide at home.

It was getting the State Health and Corrections Ministers together that secured the will to reform mental health services. Permission was given to build a hospital for forensically ill patients. Agreement to set up an Institute of Forensic Mental Health was another leap forward.

Planning began in earnest but it took time. Finally the Victorian Institute of Forensic Mental Health was set up in 1998 and the Thomas Embling Hospital was built to provide treatment for forensically ill patients.

Reforms in education were also desperate for attention. In 1975 I found the education centres in the prisons were still gazetted as primary schools. Was this a historical event as the illiteracy rates amongst prisoners were high? A qualification from HM Pentridge Prison wouldn't be useful going to a job interview.

When interviewing prisoners for classification purposes I gave them a piece of paper to write down their placement preferences. The establishment of their degree of literacy was the real question because then the teachers would know the appropriate level of assistance.

A flashback to my teaching days came when a prisoner beamed at me in the Classification Boardroom. 'Miss Lewis, what are you doing here?' he asked. I smiled at him and remembered our last encounter ten years earlier. I had taught him in Grade 6 at North Brunswick Primary School. Mario had a difficult background. Uprooted from his Italian village and transported to Australia. No English and marginal literacy skills. He struggled at school and was usually in trouble through feelings of loss, grief and lack of connections. He did not belong or fit in. 'Do you want to know what I most remember about you?' he asked. 'You taught me English and your husband wore a long purple kaftan to our Christmas party.' We folded into each other's laughter.

Mario was in prison for four years for robbery related to drugs. I listened to his story and talked about options for his placement. He struggled a bit writing down his preferences. I talked about the important role of education centres where he could make use of his time. Mario wanted to study coastal navigation. They all did. Working out drug drop-off points on the Australian coast was their fantasy.

My quandary was how to do something to get access to adult education funding. The TAFE (technical and further education) sector became the answer. In 1989 responsibility for education and vocational training programs in prisons was transferred to the State Training System. At last this was a way forward. Prison education centres became parts of TAFE Colleges across the state. Access to staffing and resources for education and vocational training programs began.

I remembered going to a graduation ceremony at Kangan College of TAFE. Watching the glow on the faces of the prisoners receiving their certificates dropped tears across my cheeks.

Spiralling prisoner numbers were a source of major concern in 1991, which was underscored by what we called 'Operation Sardine'.

There were no available prison beds and the police cells were full. I was acting Director-General of Corrections at this time and the Minister for Corrections rang. There were eighty 'greenies' on their way into custody for non-payment of fines. It was an 'anti-logging' protest. He needed a solution for a Cabinet Meeting in an hour. We were building the new medium security prison at Loddon and we were about to embark on the tree planting. My walking dictionary knowledge of the **Corrections Act 1986** came in handy. I knew we could have them on prison property in tents and they could plant the trees. He thanked me for my problem-solving skills.

The 'winter' planning quarter did result in significant structural and lasting reforms because of the network connections within government circles.

I had less success on the home front because Michael was a reluctant participant. He didn't feel connected enough, even with himself, by either the psychiatrist or me to seek or accept support offered.

The last quarter working for government was the 'spring' Competitive Quarter (1992–1997). The new era began with the election of the Kennett Government in 1992. I was travelling in France at the time and was staying in the Bastille arrondissement. I received many calls from Australia to tell me I was on a list of senior public servants who would be unacceptable to the new government. Very Kafkaesque – sentenced without knowing the charges. I had worked closely with what we called red and blue governments for fifteen years. My job was to help shape and implement government policy, whoever was elected. In that I was a model public servant.

I arrived back in Australia and reported for duty. It happened our new Director-General had supervised my social work placement at Pentridge Prison some seventeen years earlier when he was Superintendent of Pentridge. He was to tell me the news. I asked if the Minister for Corrections could tell me of my 'crime'. John told me he would take it up with the Minister. In the meantime he was happy for me to stay on with my policy, legal and research team but not as Executive Director of the Office of Corrections. I could remain on the executive. My office had been packed up for my departure in my absence. I was devastated and felt angry that this could happen to me. How could I be robbed of my job? It didn't seem fair. But I was not powerless.

My professional response to my plight was strategic. I enlisted the support of everyone. I prepared a case for the Office of Merit Protection and the Equal Opportunity Commissioner just in case I needed them. I wasn't going anywhere without a fight.

Three weeks later I was offered a position to be based at the Minister's Office to help drive the private prisons project. I felt relieved my work in Corrections could continue.

I wrote project briefs, developed performance measures and evaluated the bids. Three different private prison operators won the contracts to design, build, finance and manage three new prisons in Victoria.

Now, when I look back at this time, I see my professional self was able to cope because of the structure, order and planning that work provided.

Meanwhile at home my personal self was struggling with the effect Michael's depression had on both of us. Our demon score system of one to ten came in handy if Michael reported he was feeling anything below three. I went into strategic planning mode like being at work. I would sit on the bed with him and write a list of things he needed me to do because he was inert and immobile.

1. Leaf pluck the vineyard to expose the bunches of grapes to the sun.
2. Pay a visit to the accountant to finalise our tax return.
3. Get new tyres for the tractor.

These 'down' periods were exhausting emotionally for both of us. We were grieving about his diminished capacities when he was unable to concentrate because of the fog in his head.

My love for Michael was unconditional. In order to allow more flexibility in caring for him, I retired from the Department of Justice at the end of 1997. I would find some projects of interest as a consultant. My network of connections in Corrections and health systems soon bore fruit.

I was appointed to the Inaugural Board of the Victorian Institute of Forensic Mental Health (Forensicare) in 1998. Weekly meetings in the first year were hectic, working our way through complex issues for providing forensic mental health services in Victoria. It was gratifying work: at least mentally ill prisoners could get treatment in a hospital.

In August 1998 I was appointed to a Victorian Correctional Services Task Force to 'Review Suicide and Self Harm in the Victorian Prison System.' There had been eighteen deaths in custody between 1 August 1997 and October 1998.

The government wanted answers and an independent inquiry. The Task Force was chaired by Peter Kirby (former head of Premier and Cabinet) and included Professor Paul

Mullen and myself. Our Task Force found nine of the deaths were by hanging, four from drug overdoses, one stabbing and four from natural causes. The deaths posed many questions about risk, vulnerability and pathways to suicide. We found prisoners do not suicide solely because of their personal circumstances. They can be propelled along the continuum of suicidal action by the lack of an appropriate institutional response just as they can be protected by appropriate institutional responses. Our detailed findings were reported to the Minister for Corrections on 19 November 1998. Our report was published as a parliamentary paper six months later.

Michael was interested in the work I was doing, particularly the notion that the process of identifying risk was not enough.

The probability that a person will suicide is related to the interaction between personal vulnerabilities, the stresses placed on them by their environment and the effect of immediate triggering events. I showed him the model we developed for understanding risk and pathways to suicide.

Although Michael suffered from depression, I think he somehow divorced himself from the tag of being mentally ill and the toll this had taken on him.

During this review process I had two flashbacks because they were emotionally charged events for me. I saw a dead prisoner hanging in his cell in 1980 which took my breath away. How could anyone do this – what desperation the prisoner must have felt.

I was given the 'Hangman's Hat' worn by the prison officer who hanged Ronald Ryan. The hat was soft yet felt metallic. It was in the shape of a paper bag which the officer put over his head to avoid closely witnessing the event. A way of emotionally distancing himself from the experience. What must it have felt like for the prison officer and the prisoner.

It takes no imagination to know the prisoner was terrified. Did the prison officer distance himself and just do his job?

In time I would thank Michael for sparing me the image of seeing him hanging.

Code of Female Friendship

Surviving all that maleness from the Bluestone Decades (1975–1997) led me to wonder if there is a shared code of female friendship.

Although I made close male friends during my working life, I wondered now why women are my life's closest allies. Is there a different shared sentiment with female friendships? Why do girls and women talk about different things to boys and men?

It starts when girls are young and the intimacy close girlfriends have is like a first chaste trial marriage. Emily Bitto, the writer of *The Strays*, crystallised this idea for me where she talks about 'leg sisters' who share a bed and sleep together all tangled up. I have had three in my life.

My first leg sister was my real sister Kay whose bond is blended in the poem I wrote for her. My second leg sister was a close school friend. We not only spent all day together in class but also rode home from school on the same tram. After dinner we then spent hours talking on the telephone. We shared everything, frustrations in our lives, the heartaches, desires and wishes. The topics could range from painful menstruation and learning to use tampons to the first kiss we had experienced. Usually, deep emotions were shared. We slept in the same bed when we stayed at each other's houses.

I discovered my third leg sister at a bridge camp because

there were not enough beds. For the last twenty years a group of my women friends go to a bridge camp annually for a week to play cards, laugh and share our joys and sorrows. For five years we went to the Kangaroo Valley to a property owned by the brother of my adult leg sister. He was astonished one morning to find Jenny and me snuggled up together in the same bed. We were very close female friends who had no secrets.

The next night we found her brother had placed a balustrade in the middle of the bed so we would not be touching. Too much intimacy. Although he was gay he didn't get our platonic pleasures. We removed the balustrade.

Although Michael and I had many shared interests, I needed my own space too. My female friendship networks provided nourishment, support and encouragement because now I struggled to live with Michael and his depression.

I recently read a Danish study from the Denmark Happiness Research Institute. The findings reported that women are typically better at creating and maintaining social relationships. They also found a sense of belonging through friendship is one of the best indicators of happiness for women. This has been my experience too.

I wondered if men and boys talk about the same things as girls and women. Or are we just wired differently?

Thinking about my platonic male friends, I now realise my two long-term close male friends are gay. They both have more female attributes than blokes generally do. I have close emotional ties with them. I wondered if this is because there is never a question of a gender agenda in our friendships.

Friendship Circles

Each spring the Hinterland Scarecrow Festival is held on the Mornington Peninsula. People are invited to make exhibits and a map is published of the scarecrow trail so visitors can see the exhibits and vote for the scarecrow they like best. The prize is the People's Choice Award. The scarecrows are on display for four weeks before judging day.

Six months before Michael died I had a creative itch to build an exhibit and perused the brochure to find that in 2011 the theme was Spring Carnival.

I wonder now, what was the trigger for such a project? Maybe this was a coping mechanism for me because Michael was disintegrating in front of my outstretched arms of understanding. I asked my circle of friends to help me build a joyful scarecrow.

I had an idea to make a woman dressed in finery because she could be going to the Spring Racing Carnival. A friend suggested I build her on Arthurs Seat Road in front of our property for all to see.

Our vineyard was called Mike and Lew's Folly. I had plenty of vine canes and trunks because friends had helped me to prune the vineyard.

The project began when a friend gave me a large circular table. Two burly blokes helped me to turn the table upside down and we put a long umbrella pole in the middle of the table base. The infrastructure had to be sturdy to withstand the spring rains because the exhibits are on display for a month.

I soaked the vine canes to make them malleable. I began her crinoline, threading the vines together. Ouch. Those canes had attitude and whipped back in my face. Just like Michael because the demons were pursuing him and he was lashing out at me. The scarecrow was over a metre in height and her crinoline spanned nearly a metre wide. Her elegant dress was now taking shape. I decorated her bodice in vine leaves. I had dried the leaves out, sealed them for protection from the rains.

A friend suggested a bicycle helmet could be her face. I covered the helmet in yellow silk. Her features were made from glittering red jewels which I sewed onto the silk. Donations of brooches, earrings, beads adorned her neck. The crowning fashion touch was her large brimmed hat harnessed by red stockings.

The final touch was red cellophane balls that I poked into the bodice behind the canes.

I was away for a weekend with a group of friends when we crafted the poem and named my scarecrow. She would be called Madame L's Folly. A friend, Russell Kenery, became the lead poet.

The poem was written on red cardboard on a black placard attached to the fence behind Madame L, my scarecrow.

Scarecrow Exhibit: 'Madame L's Folly'…
Artist: Lew Wynne-Hughes
Madame L, fashionista
Posing all day
Looking too graceful

To scare birds away.
Her style is original
And wonderfully unique,
Fashioned from fields
Of vineyards boutique.
Her glorious cane dress
Is crafted from vines,
Cut from the vineyard
That makes elegant wines.
Though her Spring Festival outfit
Displays great flair,
As a scarecrow L's a folly
'Cos she just doesn't scare.

After my scarecrow won the People's Choice Award, Russell Kenery created another plaque to celebrate her winning what he called the Proletariat's Choice Award. In jest he added two paragraphs outlining what he imagined Boris Arvatov and Germaine Greer would say about Madame L's Folly.

'This work is a fine example of the Socialist Realism art form. The symbolism of "Madame L" facing away from the meticulous vineyard metaphorically rejects the folly of bourgeois attempts to impose human notions of order on Nature' – Boris Arvatov, Hinterland Festival Artistic Director and past Commissar of the Moscow and Leningrad Proletkult Union.

'Lew Wynne-Hughes is a leader of the new wave of feminist expressionism. Her sculpture, "Madam L's

Folly", interprets the scarecrow anthropomorphically as non-gender specific. It challenges the traditional testosterone driven convention that scarecrows are phallocentrist and heteropatriachalist' – Germaine Greer, Feminist, Academic, Scholar.

Madame L is still on Arthurs Seat Road in Red Hill with red geraniums growing up her backside through the canes. Over the past five years at Festival time I have made repairs to her face and her dress with help from friends. Madame L could have been me being repaired. Her sturdy infrastructure could have been my firm foundations. The repairs I made each year could be my own healing process.

It is now time for me to dismantle her. Move on and make a new, different scarecrow for the 2018 Festival.

I thanked my good friends for their support at a special dinner to celebrate Madame L's Folly's win at the Hinterland Festival.

Creating and cooking delicious dinners for friends has always been important in my life. Preparing and sharing meals with people is about love because food, for me, is a metaphor for sustenance, nourishment and enrichment. Friendship menus probably have three courses and I imagine my dad would have said what is important about friendship recipes are the ingredients in making, maintaining and nurturing friends. What a treat it is to meet someone you feel naturally connected with, whether this is via shared interests or chemistry.

What might a friendship menu look like? The ingredients and recipe for the entree might go something like this: warmth, generosity, kindness, intellect, care, shared interests and fun. Mix all the ingredients and shake well and you may find a potential friend has entered your life as a free spirit full of laughter and fun and you want more.

You liked the entree and you were still hungry. At this point provide an invite for dinner with others to share a main course. Connecting people together with interesting friends is fun, sharing exotic cuisine, complemented by beautiful wine. But it is the ingredients in particular that are the main attraction: honesty, loyalty, support, listening ears, truth, tenderness, gratitude, acceptance and nurturing.

Bake these ingredients at 180 degrees until they melt. Serve with a garnish of gratitude and loads of love and your hunger will be satisfied for the time being. But there is more to come because my dad would say effort in nurturing friends is important and that is why they stay around for dessert. Dad decided truth and acceptance are the keys in enriching friendships.

What is the essence of true friendship?

It is hard to wander into the literature of friendship without meeting the most poignant insights of two great minds: Ralph Waldo Emerson and William Shakespeare. Emerson suggests there are two elements of friendship. One is being able to speak the truth and the other is tenderness shared in friendship. He notes that trust and total magnanimity are the essence of true friendship. The message for me is about the ability to be oneself and express one's feelings, being accepted without judgements or expectations. I also love the words on friendship from Shakespeare as they strike a chord for me. A friend is someone who knows you as you are, understands where you have been, accepts what you have become and still, gently allows you to grow.

A Stepping Stone

Four and a half years after Michael died, another blow hit me. My lover of eighteen months disappeared from my life without warning. 'I was always destined to be just a stepping stone across the stream of your life. We were wonderful together,' he wrote. How had I caused this separation to happen?

Meeting my lover had been an epiphany. We had met at a library and discovered books were the beginning of our bond. I dropped a book which he rescued. 'You remind me of Stevie Nicks' was his opening line. We babbled on for ten minutes, sussing each other out. The electricity between us had started. We shared phone and address details. The next morning on my doorstep there was a CD of Fleetwood Mac. I sent him a text and so our togetherness began.

He was a scholar, an intellectual and we shared similar political views. My lover put a flower on my windscreen. He sent me articles and books. Travelling to Melbourne each week to see him made my heart sing. He held me in his arms, I loved the strength of him – this is what I needed. He awakened my body, mind and soul. He let me be. Help me here, Luctus, to understand what happened.

I told my lover casually that I'd been out with another guy three times in recent weeks. I could see from the anguish in his face, he was shutting down and pushing me away.

It does show a lack of insight on your part. Loving relationships are based on trust and honesty. How did you imagine he would react to such news? Why didn't you talk to your lover about this man before you went out with him? I would have felt pissed off too.

I'm not sure why I didn't talk to him. The other guy had been introduced by a mutual friend. His wife had died a year earlier and he was keen to meet women. I thought I was just being friendly. Or was it because sometimes I felt unsettled by my lover's love because it was risky, uncertain and I was emotionally exposed?

Three times you met this other guy. What sort of signal does this give your lover?

The wrong signal because I knew this man was not my type and I adored my gorgeous lover.

Imagine how you would have reacted if your lover had told you that he had done the same thing. Your behaviour was obviously hurtful. You obviously didn't understand the trust you had with your lover.

I felt misunderstood, but the way you explain it does make sense now. I did try to contact him but he didn't want to see me again. His note, 'We were wonderful together', kept echoing in my ears. Past tense. I really had blown it and was struggling with my new reality. Alone again. Spiralling out of control.

You need some professional help to deal with his disappearance and other losses in your life. Don't get stuck in compounding grief. You can learn from your past responses to loss.

It was through a haze of booze that I began looking on the internet for professional therapeutic help. I discovered a program called 'The Sanctuary' at Byron Bay. I made contact and had a telephone interview with the Clinical Director. She explained it was an individual holistic program for one month in a private residence on the beach. It offered extensive medical, psychological and social programs in a drug-free, confidential and caring environment. Sounded just like what I needed. I disappeared to The Sanctuary for a month.

I found it was a place of refuge and safety. I lived in a house with a carer and listened to the lapping of the waves. A walk each morning on the beach at 6 am was refreshing. The program involved therapy, massage, personal training, pilates, meditation, dancing, acupuncture, physiotherapy, and creative and narrative writing. I had a bath each night, in a candlelit bathroom, before I went to bed at 8 pm. I felt nourished by delicious home-cooked meals. It wasn't the booze I missed, but the coffee. After pleas to the medical officer I was allowed one coffee a day before noon.

Tell me what you learned about yourself. Was the experience worthwhile?

I had time to explore the work of Professor Brené Brown on the power of vulnerability. Her insights provided a new way of understanding myself. It was liberating to express my vulnerability and share my feelings with my therapist. It helped me to understand the burden of compounding grief. The Sanctuary program also introduced me to the concept of mindfulness and the value of paying attention to my senses. The staff helped me to put my jigsaw pieces back together. It felt like I was renovating myself, guided by the carers.

Seeking, hearing, smelling, touching and feeling became a way for me of getting in touch with the present. A kind of healing path through applying mindfulness in my daily life.

Awareness of body sensations rather than intellectualising everything. Exploring how I could fill my silhouette and get in touch with emotional cut-outs. Someone said mindfulness was observing without judgement and that made sense to me. Therapy sessions were sometimes tough but I did all my exercises and homework. Sessions with my psychologist forced me to be brutally honest with myself, to confront my inner struggles. I learned how to connect with my feelings by naming them and expressing them. I learned how to sit with discomfort. It was like researching me – taking a risk, emotional exposure and learning new ways to live with uncertainty. Acceptance of my imperfections and my changed reality, living with my aloneness.

I wrote a poem during a narrative writing session. Can I read it to you please and tell me what you think? Luctus was listening carefully.

A MESSAGE TO MYSELF
Here's the thing about 'inner' self
Too often neglected
Too busy 'doing' rather than 'being'
Pause
Kindness is love made visible
To self and others
Let go of self-destructive behaviours
Build on my strength muscles
Acceptance of imperfections
Awakened self
Awareness
Senses to be explored
Mindfulness
Courage to embrace vulnerability

Choice, freedom, empowerment
Authenticity and truth
Joy, belonging, creativity and connections
Purpose and meaning in life
Breathe it in
Pause
Let inner peace emerge and be.

That is lovely, you are creative with words. Have you thought about writing about your experiences? They might be helpful for others. Sometimes fresh eyes on yourself and self-reflection can be helpful to make sense of your life. The theme of aloneness keeps coming up in our conversation. What does it mean for you?

As you know, I struggled on my own. At the encouragement of friends I did try online dating for a while. This experience was humiliating in a way because I did not find intimacy and companionship. You can be alone even with another.

One guy was an alcoholic, twice divorced with five children. He was looking for a nurse to take care of him in Melbourne. Another guy was itinerant and not well off. Someone said avoid nurse and purse seekers.

My kind, caring Luctus cautioned me about thinking I needed a husband or a partner because there are plenty of people around to share in adventures. Building connections with others with shared interests might be more productive, I wondered.

Do you want me to describe how I think you are travelling? Like a report card on your emotional recovery path.

Luctus is adorable the way he listens to me and has such wisdom and insights. Those loving eyes soothe me.

Well, it seems to me you are beginning to listen to your

life. Let it speak too. Your insight about the myth of closure in the grief process was profound for you. The discovery of your sorrow pocket is a creative way to carry past pain. Well done. You seem to be getting in touch with your emotional cut-outs. Choosing emotional safety and living in the present works well for you. Keep surrounding yourself with people who know and love you. They can provide encouragement and support. Avoid people pleasing. Shift the emphasis to what you need and what makes you happy.

You seem calmer. Solitude has probably given you some emotional space. Keep up connections with people you love. Share your vulnerability with close friends. Where you live is a sanctuary and a safe haven. You will blossom again.

Letting Go

It was four years after Michael died that I started writing notes about my memories of past traumas. Fresh eyes on these quake events brought intense feelings rumbling back. Maybe I should tell Luctus about how past burdening pains have changed.

My brother Rob was tall in stature with long curly brown hair and a beard. He always wore very colourful woolly jumpers. Rob was a fine chess player even on his deathbed. He was a green thumb too. But his favourite pastime was carpentry. In his big men's shed there were life size prints of his two heroes. The first was mathematician and physicist Albert Einstein and the second was Sigmund Freud. Rob had trained as a Freudian therapist and after Rob's death Michael and I travelled to Vienna to visit Freud's rooms. It would have brought a smile to Rob's face to see me sitting on that famous couch. We had many fierce debates about the Freudian approach to therapy. My memories of my brother now focus on these positive images. I have fond memories of the fun and love we shared during the forty years of his life.

What I remember most clearly about my sister Kay is her long textured thick hair and silky white complexion. As young women we both had what we called our secret memory boxes where we kept our treasures. It had always been our plan to show the contents of our boxes to each other on our 21st birthdays, a way to remember our secrets. I opened Kay's box on her 21st birthday, two years after she died. It made me feel warm and close to her; it brought back the joy of shared memories. Inside her box I found photos of her last boyfriend. They had been keen to get married and have many children. There were love notes from boyfriends, restaurant menus and her gymnasium medals. There were a number of silver spoons and serviette rings. I smiled remembering that Kay used to pinch them from balls, parties and dinners. She called them 'souvenirs'; I call her 'Kleptomaniac Kay'.

I still have the secret box with her treasures along with her ponytail. My grief about my sister has now softened into sorrow. We were 'skin sisters', born of the same parents, and 'leg sisters' by choice for the eighteen years of her life.
I can understand now why Rob and Kay have a place in your sorrow pocket.

My feelings and memories of Michael and his demons are clearer now. I have a better understanding of why he was so desperate that he gave up on life and me. I was struck by some similarities when reading Gabrielle Carey's memoir, *In My Father's House*. Carey explores grief after her father's suicide and attempts to understand his despair. She suggests that there is still a stigma around admitting to pain and depression. It seemed to me that this is particularly so for men, like Carey's father and Michael who had been high achieving academics and researchers. Both were plagued by depression and the global financial crisis appeared to be another stepping stone along each of their paths to suicide. They both felt like failures.

Carey's father believed he was a hypocrite in his financial dealings, given his public political stance against 'the establishment' and big business opportunists. Michael believed our financial circumstances would be different if he had managed our money more wisely. He felt he was not good enough for me. My attempts to console him did not help. Michael felt unworthy and disconnected. His dark side of emotional and physical abuse at Catholic schools had left a scar too.

I also read Helen Garner's book *Everywhere I Look*. She makes this point that there is a secret darkness that lives in every one of us. Michael had a secret darkness that no one except me glimpsed.

Owning up to vulnerability was not Michael's way. Pity we were unaware of the work of Professor Brené Brown about shame and vulnerability. I think it would have helped us with his struggle.

It seems you are suggesting that you have accepted things you cannot change. An important insight in understanding your 'inner self'.

Creativity

My library has views over the vineyard and the tall trees looking back to Mornington. From here I can feel and see the seasons change and watch my whimsical garden flower and flourish. My property faces north and the library is perched on the hill near my house. It has windows on three sides and a deck. Smells from the herbs in the wine barrels on the deck come wafting into my library.

We built my decoupage studio originally in 2007. I converted it into the new Lewis Library in 2014. This project was inspired by seeing the library of a writer friend. I imagined myself being in a space totally surrounded by books, papers and writing plans. It makes my heart sing to think back now how and why I created my new personal space.

I knew I wanted the portrait of my dad as centre stage. I commissioned it for his 80th birthday present. It was painted by an artist, Micky Szilogye. I wanted this to be a feature on the western wall so my dad could look over me in my new book haven.

I drew a diagram measuring the dimensions of the portrait. The best place for the bookshelves would be around my father, from the ceiling to the floor. The whole western wall is 10 metres x 15 metres, and it could house my beloved books.

I had the entire studio stripped and found a home for the kitchen.

I had to think about the bookshelves in the library. Maybe design help would be a good idea.

I knew an interior designer, Kaye, who had redecorated my friend Melissa's place. I liked her and she had good taste. I hired her to help with my library project. Kaye showed me colours and textures. I chose a range of rustic colours. She arrived with samples and ideas so the project was underway. Paint colours were chosen and floor coverings picked. I found a cabinet-maker to build the bookshelves.

I assessed more samples. I chose custom-made red gum fiddleback shelves because I liked the grain, colour and texture of the wood.

All new furniture complemented the surrounds: rust coloured chairs and a black rustic-looking desk. Kaye brought me samples for covering the sofa. The material we chose is highly textured and looks like books on shelves.

Kaye asked me about Dad's portrait.

I had commissioned it and told Dad the artist would need to visit him a few times at home. Although Dad thought it a waste of my money, he was chuffed about his present. Micky, our artist, captured my dad's essence. The painting shows some sadness in his eyes, but it reveals his kind and honest face. His hands are telling, showing strength and resilience, and those long fingers could tell some stories. Dad is sitting in his favourite chair with his hands on the chair arms. His pale blue linen shirt is casually unbuttoned. The greys and blues of his rumpled jumper and creased pants show off the tints and shades of the lovely soft colours. This painting is a treasured possession of mine.

Dad and I are together again in my favourite space on Red Hill.

I felt connected to him putting his treasures in my library. I have a section in my library of Dad's things, like his war service medals and his coin collection. It was holding the family treasure, a copy of the *Webster's New International Dictionary of the English Language*, edition of 1926 with its 3000 pages, that saw me reaching for the tissue box. It was a gift to Dad from his father.

It took weeks to transfer all my books into the library. I divided it into sections. Art, Cooking, Travelling, Wine, Bridge, Dictionaries, Fiction and Nonfiction. I feel partnered by my books which are a comfort to me. I love sitting in my new space.

It was three years after Michael's death when my energy levels were returning that I began thinking about redecorating my living room.

It all started by accident when I bought a painting called 'Autumn Harvest' by Adelaide artist Stephen Trebilcock. It is an oil painting that is very textured and luscious and it depicts grapes and grapevines around harvest time. The artist captured the essence of autumn, my favourite season. The leaves are rust coloured and the bunches of pinot noir grapes are full, ripe and ready to be plucked. I thought it should go in the living room which looks down towards my vineyard.

The painting had been dwarfed initially on white walls

that subtracted from the beauty and vibrancy of the work. This led to another decorating project. I hired my interior designer Kaye to help me because the idea of travelling around shops looking for furniture did not appeal. I explained I wanted a warm space to complement the painting and autumnal rust colours.

Kaye had great suggestions, including wallpapering the feature wall. It reminded me of all the messy wallpapering Michael and I did in our first house in Prahran in the 1970s. We had chosen bold red colours then and papered the living room. Glue, rollers and mess. Just as well we were going to replace the floor coverings in our Prahran house.

This time the highly textured straw coloured wallpaper would be applied by an expert. Kaye brought paint samples and we decided to paint the alcoves either side of the open fireplace in a rust colour to display my decoupage pieces. I had decorated four busts that were shown at a Decoupage Guild exhibition. The images were from an Art Nouveau pack of playing cards. The male busts were spades and clubs and the female busts were diamonds and hearts. The design was tricky as the busts were contoured in the shape of male and female bodies. Michael had helped me with the mathematics for this project. Now at night my decoupage pieces are shown off because the lamps behind them have created a symmetrical glow in the rust alcoves.

Kaye and I decided to replace all the furniture in the living room, including the chair Michael had died in. The furniture hunt in Melbourne with Kaye turned out to be easy because she did all the legwork. My rust coloured leather reading chair came first, and then the old burnt umber coloured Chinese altar table. The chairs, couch and cushions were matched in autumnal colours. Now at night with the fire blazing, my painting 'Autumn Harvest' talks to me and glows. We are connected.

The decorating projects were about renewal, investing the emotional energy back into my life again. In the process of redecorating my home, I was discovering there were advantages to not being partnered.

There is no need to consult, compromise or negotiate. The other advantage of being single is the total autonomy it brings. I could choose how to use my time, even staying up all night reading if I felt like it. It also allows me to get together with friends who share interests, yet enjoy solitude's clarifying lens.

I discovered that cooking was another joyful frontier of creativity. A friend, Jenny, gave me a cookbook by Ottolenghi. This led to my cooking renaissance, lovingly preparing meals to share with friends. Ottolenghi's food philosophy is simple – use the freshest ingredients available and interfere as little as possible with the food. Simplicity in food preparation is the key and keeping refrigeration to a minimum, particularly with salads. These must be fresh, otherwise their textures and flavours are destroyed.

One morning I opened my front door to find the front step laden – a hessian bag of garlic, oranges and lemons and a bag of tomatoes. There was no note. The front doorstep is a wondrous place to discover things left for me. Kind gestures.

With the goodies left on my doorstep I cooked a

dinner using Ottolenghi's recipes. It started with Labneh, an Arab cheese made by straining yoghurt until it loses most of its liquid. Rolling this into balls and coating them in sumac powder gave a sharp acidic thrust. The main course was seared duck, blood oranges and star anise. The cumin, fennel seeds and chillies made it so flavoursome combined with the oranges. Ottolenghi uses spices simply but creatively, and the display of the food reveals colours and textures. I served this with his famous pomegranate and tomato salad which glistens and beams of flavours. I shared this meal with my 'doorstep' friends.

Partnering

In the year before Michael died, I often went to social events by myself because he didn't want to go.

Friends organised a dinner at Bittern Cottage, a local restaurant, and I was sitting at a table with strangers. It didn't take long before the couple sitting opposite were introduced as Jenny Platt, the lawyer, and Sandy Webb, the scientist. They were professional women of a similar age with outgoing personalities. They had just moved to Red Hill. We started talking about books and what we liked to read.

The conversation then turned to book clubs as I was setting one up in Red Hill. Jenny wanted to know how they worked. I shared my different experiences of the two book clubs I had belonged to. The first time I joined one was in the '70s. The books were supplied by the Council of Adult Education and we didn't necessarily receive our first choice, which was disappointing. This was not the main frustration. The group consisted of young mothers, talking about breastfeeding and colic. It seemed like hours before the book got a guernsey. It was boring. I finally resigned.

In contrast the second Bookworm Book Club worked well because of the protocols developed by Jenny Armstrong, who set up the book club. These included that we would start on time. The chair, who had chosen the book for discussion, would prepare the questions and facilitate discussion. This was my kind of club. It was organised and focused which probably says something about my emotional need for structure and certainty. Made me wonder about my career path in prisons. Order, structure, planning and containment. Fresh eyes on myself.

One hot summer night we had all read *A Suitable Boy* by Vikram Seth. At its core the novel is about a mother struggling to find a suitable boy for her daughter to marry. We had a brilliant discussion about the questions posed in the book. All laughing and drinking. One of our members then started talking about what makes a boy unsuitable or suitable. Jane suggested we should think of boys as either 'stilettos' or 'slippers'. Jane went on to explain she had a choice of whom she married. Jane's stiletto was a doctor, a womaniser and high risk on a number of levels and her slipper was a lawyer who had been head prefect at Scotch College, reliable and trustworthy and not high risk. She married the slipper, the suitable boy. So around the table we went sharing our own stories.

It was 2 am in the morning and we were still going strong until the husband of the hostess appeared at the top of the stairs with a pillow around his head, telling us where we could all go. We waited ten minutes for him to go back to bed and we started up again. Most of us had married unsuitable boys in the eyes of our parents, with Catholics teaming up with Protestants.

Michael was an unsuitable boy in the eyes of my mother.

He had been brought up Catholic, he had introduced me to left wing radicals and professors and was often barefooted. You might have guessed Michael was a stiletto. I would never have teamed up with a predictable slipper because I love eccentricity and quirkiness in others and myself.

Jenny, my new friend, laughed and was pleased when I invited her to join the Blue Stocking Book Club in Red Hill. We could start our club with protocols and agree on how we would conduct our meetings. 'Why are book clubs so popular?' Jenny asked. We can share our ideas about the books and listen and learn from each other. We can foster friendship and respect for the views of others. We are all partnered by books.

My affair with books began when I was a child, when my parents read me bedtime stories. Now books are my refuge and haven. Books are like companions. Books stop me feeling alone because they are like partners you can love. You can savour the thoughts.

After Jenny and I finished talking about books, I asked her out of the blue if she played bridge. I wonder what gave me this clue. Jenny was an intelligent, professional woman with a sparkle in her eyes. Probably good at games, I thought. We both bubbled with delight because we talked about bridge, books, bidding systems and bridge conventions.

Bridge is like a language that you need to learn together. Bridge books outline systems and knowledge about play. But understanding what your partner is telling you in the bidding is the key. A silent shared language. If you give wrong information to your partner, their response will not be right. A bit like clear communication in a partnership based on trust and reliability.

It was not long before Jenny and I started playing each Monday morning at the Flinders Bridge Club. We have continued this partnership since. Our Monday morning ritual begins with a drive to Flinders. I love coming over the hill looking out to Phillip Island. The vista over the ocean is so calming. We then walk around the Flinders Golf Course before a coffee at the cafe. It's a great start to the week because we then play twenty-four hands of competitive duplicate bridge.

The bridge club is run by an energetic couple, Peter and Felicity Laine. After each session we receive the results of the day. Jenny and I get together to analyse how we played and to discuss where we could have performed better. We want to improve our partnership and learn together.

I love the ambience of the club, and the other bridge colleagues have become my bridge family. One Monday morning, another bridge friend said, 'You look like a symphony of colour because you always turn up in colourful hats and stockings.' It then became a playground for me, knowing I would be scrutinised each week to see how outrageous I could look. Roy Potter, our oldest bridge player, always makes a beeline for me and I make him laugh. One morning I wore my koala hat with whiskers which sent him into gales of laughter.

I provided the colour at our Christmas party this year. I wore my heavily jewelled rainbow coloured leggings. Roy sat at our table and wanted to know when I bought them. They are my hysterectomy pants because Michael gave them to me as a hysterectomy present. Roy and the team of players just laughed. I was discovering my quirkiness and being a 'show-off' was my way. It brought out smiling faces.

One Monday morning I was talking to my cousin over the bridge table after her recent trip to Turkey, a group trip with Sarah Stegley of 'The Inspired Traveller' fame. I was listening carefully because Sarah was a friend of ours from decades ago. My cousin lent me a book, *The Museum of Innocence* by Orhan Pamuk, which she said was a must as pre-reading if I wanted to go to Turkey. I wondered what a group trip would be like.

I feared travelling alone; the idea did not appeal to me. Why? I asked myself. Needy me, always in search of connections with people. I had lived in the safety of home with my parents before I met Michael. Although it was a safe and loving place, our family members were not openly affectionate with each other. As a child living with the stigma of epilepsy, I had emotionally packaged myself up and learned how to seek approval from others, even though I was a bit shy. Being good at sport helped with developing friendships. I used to think of myself as a bit of a 'church mouse'. My confidence grew during adolescence but I was shy when I met Michael. I was always more outgoing and comfortable with a few drinks. When Michael and I teamed up, the drinking pattern began. Michael and I were a very affectionate couple for our first few years together until his first affair. Over time I became emotionally distant in some ways. Probably because his affairs were hurtful. Maybe we stayed together after his affairs because I did not want to be on my own. Losing my sister and brother bonded me closer to Michael. Maybe it was a way to protect myself against the pain of loss.

I wondered if my need to be connected to people and my quest to belong stemmed from loss in my life.

After Michael died I did seek people out to fill the void in my life and I still do. My curious nature wants to explore and travel, but not by myself.

I went on the group trip to Turkey.

Joining up with fellow travelling gypsies turned out to be what I needed at the time. The highlight was a hot air balloon experience over Cappadocia. We rose at 5 am to go to the balloon launching station. Up, up and away, one hundred large colourful balloons took off. The sky was decorated with delight. Cappadocia is an extinct volcano and the landscape is geographically unique. The rock formations are called 'fairy penguins' but they look phallic, like erect penises. It felt like being on and seeing another planet. Connections with Australians in foreign countries are always comforting. Our Australian pilot had flapping flags of kangaroos tied to our balloon. We arrived safely as those big balloons deflated, back on the ground. We sat there marvelling because the experience was overwhelming.

Bit like me really, the highs and lows of trying to make sense of my life. It will probably be a never-ending quest to understand myself. Do I need more research about myself because my shared journey through loss and grief has been an emotional meander not an intellectual trudge? My automatic pilot has previously been my brain not my heart or emotions. Heart bits I have found hard. There I struggle for certainty.

Before the trip to Turkey I read Orhan Pamuk's novel

The Museum of Innocence and visited the museum inspired by the book, which was awarded the Nobel Prize for Literature. In *The Museum of Innocence*, Pamuk describes how Kemal collects his lover's belongings and the logic behind how he sets them out in the museum. These objects embody daily life in Istanbul during the second half of the 20th century and are displayed in the museum in carefully designed boxes and cabinets. One entire wall is 4213 cigarette butts of Kemal's lover.

I am in my library looking at the book cover, wondering how Kemal must have felt when his lover of eight years went off and married someone else. Heartbroken by the pain of lost love, I imagine.

After Michael died, it wasn't the gloom at home that I found difficult to cope with but it was touching and smelling his possessions. His books, gardening gloves and tools that brought back memories. Friends could sense I was at a low ebb. Highs and lows, and some days the sads arrived unannounced without any particular trigger. It is a mystery really. My doorstep lifted my spirits. One day I found a book by Peter Cundall of ABC fame, *The Practical Australian Gardener*. It was from my garden mentor, Wendy Fleetwood. The layout of the book describes seasonal garden tasks for each month of the year.

It encouraged some structure and order of things for me to do in the garden. Wendy would arrive each week in gardening gear to work with me. My thirst for knowledge was quenched. Finding out the red hellebores did best in part shade under deciduous trees was an insight. Understanding nature, nurture and position seem to be the ingredients of marriage in the garden. Wendy listened to my pain as we nattered. Getting my hands dirty in the red soil gave me sustenance somehow. It was soothing.

As the months wore on we seeded a plan to design and build the infrastructure for a half-moon herb garden. Those lovely rocks are the border. All my favourite herbs smell delicious and the textures are furry. The red and purple salvias stand up and send me messages that they are happy. My quest to grow petunias and sweet peas then began. The sweet peas always remind me of my happy childhood. My favourites are the reds and purples. Sweet peas have attitude – they climb up the maypole and trellis and they say 'pick me and I will keep coming'. They start dancing in early spring and last through to summer. I make sweet pea posies for my friends.

The Scarlet O'Hara petunias are a mix of rosy red and royal purple. They live in my French oak wine barrels on the deck. Patty, my petunia friend, and I compare notes and read up about tending the petunias, celebrating these gifts from nature and sharing stories. Engaging with nature is a way of coping for me.

Finding

Luctus wanted to talk to me about his observations of my journey through loss and grief. I was listening carefully.

Friendship has been the force that powered your survival. And what fostered your life as you emerged from darkness? Three pleasures: gardening, cooking and design changes to your home.

Looking at the pages that describe your joys you must understand that others might think they were all human doings rather than human beings. They are wrong. Each passion was engaged with creatively. They expressed your existence. Your pursuits in the kitchen or garden or rooms in your home were each embraced with a passion that was a wonderful part of who you are and not just what you were doing.

Your reclaimed audacity, creativity, humour and flair coloured all you did as you reached for a different life, your existence without Michael. They took your arms and placed them around life-affirming pleasures as they pulled your hands away from booze bottles. And they produced things that were living symbols of a fresh life that surrounded you and gave pleasure to others.

Ashes to Ashes

Michael was passionate about his footy team, Geelong, also known as the Mighty Cats. He also had a similar passion for our lilac Burmese cat, Lily. She was with him, curled up on his lap, when I found him on that fateful Tuesday. Lily was to be part of the ritual at the scattering of Michael's ashes.

It was the third anniversary of Michael's death. His wish was for his ashes to be scattered in our vineyard. It was a warm, sunny December afternoon. I was dressed in my favourite red frock and wearing red, yellow and blue striped stockings. My red akubra hat protected me from the sun. Some fifty friends and family had come to my place to say our final farewell to Michael.

My friend Wendy had given me a rainbow banner to mark the occasion. The three different sized red circles were attached to a long black stick. Inside the circles were strips of colourful material. The circles whirled around in the wind. I held the banner high when we headed down the hill to the vineyard, located some few hundred metres from my house. The occasion did not go as planned. Laugh at me and laugh with me.

Lily came on the walk with us, rubbing up against my legs which she loves to do. Lily thought it was just like old times. She was always with Michael when he was tending our vines. Lily would sit on the timber posts that hold up the wires and the canopy of the vine canes. As Michael worked along the row of canes, she would hide amongst the leaves and then pounce on his shoulders. It was like hide and seek. Lily never tired of this game in the vineyard, nor did Michael.

I placed the banner in the pinot noir plot where we were to sprinkle the ashes. I opened the box and a dozen friends each took a handful of ashes. As we started scattering the ashes, Lily rolled in them. She thought it was a new vineyard game. The more we scattered, the more Lily rolled. She also thought it was kitty litter.

We all burst into gales of laughter, hugging each other and clapping at Lily's performance. We should have had the Geelong footy team theme song playing. Michael would have loved his last hoorah and Lily's role in it. Luctus was standing by me and laughing with us. Lily was snuggled in my arms. We were surrounded by the love of my friends. The red earth felt solid under my feet again. The scattering of Michael's ashes was about shedding my grief and understanding that how I reacted to loss was my way.

We ambled up the hill to my house, passing my beautiful red tree. I will decorate it this Christmas with some more ornaments of the tree of life and a big red star.

I feel anchored.

About the Author

If you saw me skipping down the street you'd probably smile. Clad in my strawberry hat, red garb and red shoes you'd guess this 68-year-old woman was a colourful quirky creature.

And you'd never imagine I worked in prisons for three decades as a social worker, senior correctional administrator and consultant. But I did. This prison environment provided some seeds for my understanding of mental illness, loss and grief. My work in Corrections was my passion.

I matured in Melbourne with my brothers and sister in a close-knit middle-class family. My father was a newsagent with a thriving book business. My mother was an artist. They got on. My affection for books and creativity began as a child and has chased me ever since.

The institutions that tried to shape my education were Methodist Ladies' College, Toorak Teachers' College, Monash University (social work) and Melbourne University (criminology).

With my husband Michael I found sanctuary late in my life in Red Hill on the Mornington Peninsula. Together we followed our dream to establish a vineyard and make our own wine. This pleasure continued until Michael's wretched death in 2011.

Grieving for my beloved Michael after his suicide enabled multiple family traumas of disappearance, heartache and death to unfold. The layering effect of my grieving helped with my struggle to make sense of the loss of Michael.

Silhouette of Sorrow is my first book. It is a shared journey through loss and grief.

www.ingramcontent.com/pod-product-compliance
Lightning Source LLC
Chambersburg PA
CBHW042132160426
43199CB00021B/2887